P

Integration and Human Rights

Peace Integration and Human Rights

SHAYKH-UL-ISLAM
Dr MUHAMMAD TAHIR-UL-QADRI

Author: Dr Muhammad Tahir-ul-Qadri

Published by
Minhaj Publications India Forum
Umaj Road, At & Post : Karjan - 391240
Dist. Vadodara, Gujarat
India

All proceeds from the books, literature and audio-visual media (all multimedia) delivered by Dr Muhammad Tahir-ul-Qadri are entirely donated to Minhaj-ul-Quran International (MQI).

A catalogue record for this book is available from the British Library.
ISBN–13: 978–1–908229–19–9

www.minhaj.org | www.minhajuk.org | www.minhaj.in
www.minhajpublications.com |_www.minhajproductions.in

First Published January 2016
Printed by -Minhaj Publications India Forum
Production Unit -1 :130/582, Bakarganj, Kanpur - 208023,U. P. India

بِسْمِ اللَّهِ الرَّحْمَٰنِ الرَّحِيمِ

In the name of God, Most Compassionate, Ever-Merciful

Saying of God ﷻ

﴿يَهْدِي بِهِ ٱللَّهُ مَنِ ٱتَّبَعَ رِضْوَٰنَهُۥ سُبُلَ ٱلسَّلَٰمِ﴾

﴿By this Allah guides those who seek His pleasure to the paths to peace (and security).﴾

[Qur'ān 5:16]

Saying of the Prophet ﷺ

عَنْ فَضَالَةَ بْنِ عُبَيْدٍ ﷺ أَنَّ رَسُولَ اللهِ ﷺ قَالَ: «اَلْمُؤْمِنُ مَنْ أَمِنَهُ النَّاسُ عَلَى أَنْفُسِهِمْ وَأَمْوَالِهِمْ».

Fuḍāla b. ʿUbayd ﷺ reported that Allah's Messenger ﷺ said, "The true believer [*muʾmin*] is he whom people trust with regard to their lives and their properties".

[Aḥmad b. anbal and Ibn Mājah]

Shaykh-ul-Islam Dr Muhammad Tahir-ul-Qadri

Shaykh-ul-Islam Dr Muhammad Tahir-ul-Qadri was born in 1951 in the city of Jhang, Pakistan, hailing from a family of Islamic saints, scholars and teachers. His formal religious education was initiated in Medina at the age of 12 in Madrasa al-ʿUlūm al-Sharʿiyya, a traditional school situated in the blessed house of the Companion of the Prophet Muhammad ﷺ, Abū Ayyūb al-Anṣārī ؓ. He completed the traditional studies of classical and Arabic sciences under the tutelage of his father and other eminent scholars of the time. He continued to travel around the Islamic world in the pursuit of sacred knowledge, and studied under many famous scholars of Mecca, Medina, Syria, Baghdad, Lebanon, the Maghreb, India and Pakistan, and received around five hundred authorities and chains of transmission from them in hadith and classical Islamic and spiritual sciences. Amongst them is an unprecedented, unique and highly honoured chain of authority which connects him, through four teachers, to al-Shaykh ʿAbd al-Razzāq, the son of al-Shaykh ʿAbd al-Qādir al-Jīlānī al-Ḥasanī al-Ḥusaynī (of Baghdad), al-Shaykh al-Akbar Muḥyī al-Dīn b. ʿArabī [(the author of *al-Futūḥāt al-Makkiyya*) (Damascus)] and Imam Ibn ajar al-ʿAsqalānī, the great hadith authority of Egypt. Through another chain he is linked to Imam Yūsuf b. Ismāʿīl al-Nabhānī directly via only one teacher. His chains of transmission are published in two of his *thabts* (detailed lists):

al-Jawāhir al-Bāhira fī al-Asānīd al-Ṭāhira and *al-Subul al-Wahabiyya fī al-Asānīd al-Dhahabiyya.*

In the academic sphere, Dr Qadri received a First Class Honours Degree from the University of the Punjab in 1970. After earning his MA in Islamic studies with University Gold Medal in 1972 and achieving his LLB in 1974, Dr Qadri began to practise law in the district courts of Jhang. He moved to Lahore in 1978 and joined the University of the Punjab as a lecturer in law and completed his doctorate in Islamic Law. He was later appointed as a professor of Islamic Law and was head of the department of Islamic legislation for LLM.

Dr Qadri was also a jurist advisor to the Federal Shariat Court and Appellate Shariah Bench of the Supreme Court of Pakistan and advisor on the development of Islamic Curricula to the Federal Ministry of Education. Within a short span of time, Dr Qadri emerged as one of the Pakistan's leading Islamic jurists and scholars and one of the world's most renowned and leading authorities on Islam. A prolific author, researcher and orator, Dr Qadri has written around one thousand books, of which more than four hundred and fifty have been published, and has delivered over six thousand lectures (in Urdu, English and Arabic) on a wide range of subjects.

In 2010, Shaykh-ul-Islam Dr Muhammad Tahir-ul-Qadri issued his historic and world-renowned fatwa on the critical matter of suicide bombings and terrorism carried out in the name of Islam. It has been regarded as a significant and historic step, the first time that such an explicit and unequivocal decree against the perpetrators of terror has been broadcast so widely. The original fatwa was written in Urdu, and amounts to 600 pages of research and references from the Qur'ān, hadith, the opinions of the Companions ﷺ, and the widely accepted classical texts of Islamic scholarship. This historic work has been published in English, Indonesian and Hindi, while translation into Arabic, Norwegian, Danish, Spanish, French and other major languages is also in process. The Islamic Research Academy of Jamia al-Azhar Egypt wrote a detailed description of the fatwa and verified its contents. It gained worldwide media attention and acclaim as an indispensable tool in the intellectual and ideological struggle against violent extremism.

Also Dr Qadri is the founder and head of Minhaj-ul-Quran International (MQI), an organisation with branches and centres in more than ninety countries around the globe; he is the chairman of the Board of Governors of Minhaj University Lahore, which is chartered by the Government of Pakistan; he is the founder of Minhaj Education Society, which has established more than 600 schools and colleges in Pakistan; and he is the chairman of Minhaj Welfare Foundation, an organization involved in humanitarian and social welfare activities globally.

Dr Qadri has spent his life, and especially the last decade, in an indefatigable effort to counter religious extremism and promote peace and harmony between communities. His painstaking research into the Qur᾽ān, hadith and classical Islamic authorities has resulted in landmark works, some published, and others soon to be published, demonstrating Islam as a religion that not only safeguards human rights, but promotes peace, tolerance and socioeconomic progress. He has travelled extensively to lecture at the invitation of government and non-government agencies, and has organised and took part in international conferences in order to promote peace. He has arrayed spiritual and educational training programmes across the Western world with a focus on addressing the roots of religious extremism. He is recognised for his commitment to interfaith dialogue, with over 12,000 people attending his Peace for Humanity Conference in 2011, probably the largest interfaith gathering ever held in the UK, and which announced the London Declaration, a charter for world peace, signed online by a quarter of a million people. He has been politically active in his native Pakistan, organising massive pro-democracy and anti-corruption demonstrations. When not travelling, he is based in Canada, busy in his research activities and producing vital works of Islamic scholarship relevant to Muslims in this day and age.

Transliteration Key

ا/آ/ى	ā	ظ	ẓ
ب	b	ع	ʿ
ت	t	غ	gh
ث	th	ف	f
ج	j	ق	q
ح	ḥ	ك	k
خ	kh	ل	l
د	d	م	m
ذ	dh	ن	n
ر	r	ه	h
ز	z	و	w/ū
س	s	ي	y/ī
ش	sh	ة	a
ص	ṣ	ء	ʾ
ض	ḍ	أ	a
ط	ṭ	إ	i

Formulaic Arabic Expressions

﷾ (*Subḥānahū wa taʿālā*) an invocation to describe the Glory of Almighty Allah: 'the Exalted and Sublime'

ﷺ (*Ṣalla-llāhu ʿalayhi wa ālihī wa sallam*) an invocation of God's blessings and peace upon the Prophet Muhammad and his family: 'God's blessings and peace be upon him and his family'

⁕ (*ʿAlayhis-salām*) an invocation of God's blessings and peace upon a Prophet or an angel: 'May peace be upon him'

⁕ (*ʿAlayhas-salām*) an invocation of God's blessings and peace upon a Prophet's mother, wife, daughter and other pious woman: 'May peace be upon her'

⁕ (*ʿAlayhimas-salām*) an invocation of God's blessings and peace upon two Prophets or two angels: 'May peace be upon both of them'

⁕ (*ʿAlayhimus-salām*) an invocation of God's blessings and peace upon three or more Prophets: 'May peace be upon them'

⁕ (*Raḍiya-llāhu ʿanhu*) an invocation of God's pleasure with a male Companion of the Prophet: 'May God be pleased with him'

⁕ (*Raḍiya-llāhu ʿanhā*) an invocation of God's pleasure with a female Companion of the Prophet: 'May God be pleased with her'

⁕ (*Raḍiya-llāhu ʿanhumā*) an invocation of God's pleasure with two Companions of the Prophet: 'May God be pleased with both of them'

⁕ (*Raḍiya-llāhu ʿanhum*) an invocation of God's pleasure with more than two Companions of the Prophet: 'May God be pleased with them'

Contents

Foreword 1

Part One

Peace, Integration and Human Rights (In the Light of Qur'ān and Sunna) 5

1.1 Introduction 7
1.2 Arabia at the Time of the Prophet ﷺ 7
1.3 The Prophetic Movement began with the Revolutionary Message of Knowledge 8
1.4 The Message of Social Justice, Social Cohesion, Human Dignity and Equality 9
1.4.1 The Pioneering Nature of the Prophetic Message 10
1.5 Examples of Patience, Forbearance, Tolerance and Forgivingness in the Prophet's Character 12
1.6 Migration to Medina 15
1.6.1 The First Prophetic Sermon in Medina 15
1.6.2 The First Step in the State of Medina: Establishing Informal Socioeconomic Stability 17
1.6.3 The First Constitution in Human History: The Constitution of Medina 18

1.7 Constitutional History: A Comparative Glance 18
1.7.1 The British Constitution 18
1.7.2 The US Constitution 19
1.7.3 The Medinan Constitution 19
1.7.3.1 Religious Freedom and the Historic Condemnation of Terrorism and Acts of Violence against Non-Muslims 21
1.8 Women's Rights: A Comparative Overview 22
1.8.1 Taliban do not Represent an Islamic Government 22
1.8.2 Women's Rights in the West 23
1.8.2.1 Development of Women's Rights in Britain 23
1.8.2.2 Development of Women's Rights in the US 23
1.8.2.3 Development of Women's Rights in France 24
1.8.2.4 Women's Right to Vote in Various Other Countries 24
1.8.3 Women's Rights in Islamic Law Fourteen Centuries Ago 25
1.8.4 Muslim Women Held Prominent Roles in Early Islamic History 26
1.9 Muslim and Non-Muslim Relations 31
1.9.1 Capital Punishment Awarded to a Muslim for Murdering a Non-Muslim 32
1.9.2 The Prophet ﷺ Honoured His Christian Guests 32

1.9.3 Forgiveness of the Former Oppressors of Muslims at the Bloodless Conquest of Mecca 33
1.9.4 Islamic Law Prescribes Justice and Equity for Non-Muslims 35
1.9.5 The Blood Money (*Diyya*) of a Non-Muslim is Equal to That of a Muslim 36
1.9.6 Social Benefits and Income Support For Jobless, Old, Or Disabled Non-Muslims Living in an Islamic State 37
1.9.7 Jews and Christians Enjoyed a Multicultural Coexistence in Muslim Lands 38
1.10 The Treaty of udaybiyya: A Shining Symbol of the Prophetic Preference for Peace over Conflict 40
1.11 The West and Muslim Minorities 42
1.11.1 Understanding and Tackling Extremism and Terrorism 42
1.11.2 Muslims: Integration, Isolation, or Annihilation 42
1.11.3 Closing: The Prophet's Final Sermon—A Forerunner to the Universal Declaration of Human Rights 43

Part Two

Renouncing Terror, Regaining Peace, and the Future of Islam 45

2.1 Author's Preface 47

2.2 Lexical and Technical Meanings of Islam, *Īmān*, and *Iḥsān* 47
2.3 The Concept of Balance in Islam 55
2.4 A Detailed Exposition of the Meanings of Jihad: A Refutation of Misinterpretations 65
2.5 Historic Existence of Extremists and Terrorists in the Form of the Kharijite 70
2.6 Prophetic Biography (*sīra*) as a Model for the Umma's Success 73
2.7 Closing Words: The True Way Forward for Muslims 75

Part Three A

Islam, Peace and Democracy 77

3.1 Etymology of the Arabic Word Islam 79
3.2 Seven-Point Social Policy Formulated by the Holy Prophet ﷺ 80
3.3 The First Public Friday Address Delivered by The Holy Prophet ﷺ to The People Of Medina 81
3.4 Brief Examination of the Constitution Delivered by the Holy Prophet ﷺ 82
3.4.1 Opening Articles 83
3.4.2 Freedom of Religion 84
3.4.3 Forbiddance of Bloodshed 87
3.4.4 Protection of Human Life 88
3.4.5 Right of Privacy 92
3.4.6 Right of Equality 92
3.4.7 Guarantee of Legal Justice 93
3.4.8 Guarantee of Free-Trial 94

3.4.9 Defence of the State of Medina 94

Part Three B

Al-Hidayah Europe 2009: Question & Answer Session (UK) 97

Q1. Regarding whether Terrorism is Caused by Factors within Islam or outside Islam 99

Q2. Regarding the Prospect of Muslims Supporting Terrorism 100

Q3. Regarding the Misuse of the Blasphemy Law against Pakistani Christians 102

Q4. Regarding advice to Western Governments 104

Q5. Regarding a Research Path to Follow for Promoting the Positive Coexistence of Muslims in UK Society 105

Bibliography 109

Foreword

Young Muslims in the West and in the Islamic heartlands face many questions connected to the spread of a relatively new Kharijite philosophy, which presents a half sawn-off distorted model of Islam as the representative voice. Although the current Muslim situation is full of challenges, it is also an opportunity to present Islam, with all its intellectual rigours and spiritual intricacies, to Muslims and non-Muslims alike.

This role can only be performed by an informed leadership, whose vision is multi-dimensional; rooted in the Islamic intellectual and spiritual tradition, but at the same time aware of the modern world and the spectrum of ideologies which mould it.

The present volume is a collection of transcripts from lectures delivered by Shaykh-ul-Islam Dr Muhammad Tahir-ul-Qadri, an internationally renowned authority on the sciences of Islam, a former professor of law, and a close student of contemporary academia and the modern world. Whilst not delivered as a series, the themes running through all of these speeches are interrelated and particularly relevant to Western Muslims in the modern age.

In *Peace, Integration & Human Rights*, Shaykh-ul-Islam Dr Muhammad Tahir-ul-Qadri presents the life of the Prophet Muhammad ﷺ as the ultimate model for nurturing peace and harmony in a diverse world beckoning for a solution. This unique and unprecedented lecture bridges the Prophetic example (Sunna) with the challenges faced by western Muslims living as minorities. Some of the distinguished features gleaned from the Prophet's life include: the migration to the Illuminated City of Medina; the Constitution of Medina as the first written constitution in human history; the mechanisms used by the Prophet ﷺ to establish a culture of peace and security, knowledge and learning, human rights and equality, and socio-political prosperity; the historic treaty of udaybiyya; women's rights; the Prophet's governance of a multi-cultural society; and the Prophet's relations with non-Muslims.

In *Renouncing Terror Regaining Peace*, Shaykh-ul-Islam begins with a linguistic and theological analysis of key tenants of Islamic faith, including Islam (submission), *īmān* (faith) and *iḥsān* (excellence). Shaykh-ul-Islam Dr Muhammad Tahir-ul-Qadri then eloquently describes Prophetic teachings, which uphold the principle of peace and denounce violence and terror in all their possible manifestations. The much misunderstood concept of jihad is authoritatively unlocked, beginning with an etymological analysis of the term, followed by its implications in Islamic law. In closing, some possible root causes of extremism in the Muslim world are highlighted alongside a practical course of action anchored in the Qur'ān and the Sunna of the Prophet ﷺ.

Also included in this collection is a *Question and Answer Session* from the UK's annual al-Hidayah Europe retreat. Questions were asked by academics, researchers, a Christian representative, and a journalist. The session addresses many of the previously mentioned topics such as terrorism, integration of Muslim minorities, the West's role in ensuring a peaceful relationship with the Muslim world and more such as the misapplication of blasphemy laws in lands where Christians are minorities.

It is the sincere hope of the editors and everyone else involved in the publication of this work that the reader's understanding of Islam is deepened and rectified by this compilation. It is also hoped that this humble effort may go a long way in bringing an end to the systematic indoctrination of young Muslims here in the West and in the Muslim heartlands, as well as improving the relationship between Islam and the West.

Part One

Peace, Integration and Human Rights (In the Light of Qur'ān and Sunna)

1.1 Introduction

Life today is profoundly different to life in sixth century Arabia. The social, economic and political scenes have changed in manifold ways vis-à-vis the situation fourteen centuries ago. Every aspect of life, in both the individual and collective spheres has undergone radical change. Despite this then, why do Muslims the world-over continue to believe that the Prophet Muhammad ﷺ and his teachings transcend the vicissitudes of time and are adoptable in today's world. It is essential that this question be addressed in a manner that will remove the confusions of the modern Muslim, as well as provide a deepened understanding to those outside the sphere of Islam.

1.2 Arabia at the Time of the Prophet ﷺ

When one studies a personality or the teachings it propagated, it is essential that they appreciate the context and material circumstances surrounding them. Arabia, in the Prophet's time, was fraught with animosity and enmity. Decades old cycles of killings and revenge between tribes were commonplace. Society was bereft of all moral precepts, and human and social values. The whole region was engulfed by an atmosphere of violence and tyranny. Drinking was rife; women were treated as sexual objects, forced to dance naked at parties and festivals; female infanticide was an accepted norm; prejudices, bigotry and rancour had torn the fabric of society, whilst lofty traits of virtue, such as truth and generosity, benevolence and compassion, were conspicuously absent. The poor and destitute were considered the bane of society and were thus publicly humiliated. Widows were considered the property of their sons and in many tribes were inherited and divided along with the other property.

1.3 The Prophetic Movement began with the Revolutionary Message of Knowledge

The great civilisations of the Greeks, Egyptians, Indians, Romans and Persians had perished. Time had rendered their influences almost insignificant. Europe and the Christian world at large had fallen deep into the dark ages of religious wars and schism. Amidst such extreme global circumstances, the Prophetic light of Muhammad ﷺ shone forth. He was sent to an Arabia steeped in ignorance, and moral and spiritual restlessness. The Arabs to whom he was sent were illiterate, proud only of their photographic memories and their eloquence. As such, the fundamental teachings of the Prophet Muhammad ﷺ highlighted the importance of knowledge. He brought to Arabia an egalitarian civilisation and an enriched culture anchored in the word of God, the Qur'ān, and his own way of life, the Sunna.

The Prophetic movement began with the message of knowledge, education and the intimate connection of man to his Lord. The first revelation was a command to the Prophet ﷺ with these words:

﴿ٱقْرَأْ بِٱسْمِ رَبِّكَ ٱلَّذِى خَلَقَ ۝١ خَلَقَ ٱلْإِنسَـٰنَ مِنْ عَلَقٍ ۝٢
ٱقْرَأْ وَرَبُّكَ ٱلْأَكْرَمُ ۝٣ ٱلَّذِى عَلَّمَ بِٱلْقَلَمِ ۝٤ عَلَّمَ ٱلْإِنسَـٰنَ مَا لَمْ
يَعْلَمْ﴾

﴾*Read in the Name of your Lord, who created. He created man from a hanging mass (clinging) like a leech (in the mother's womb). Read and your Lord is Most Generous. He taught man by the pen. He taught man what he knew not.*﴿

1.4 The Message of Social Justice, Social Cohesion, Human Dignity and Equality

Countering the base social behaviour prevalent in sixth century Arabia, the divine revelation expounded the dignity of the human being and his esteemed position above the rest of creation.

﴿وَلَقَدْ كَرَّمْنَا بَنِيٓ ءَادَمَ﴾

﴾*And we have indeed ennobled the children of Adam.*﴿[1]

In addition to this, society and social stability were of utmost significance in the message propagated by the Prophet Muhammad ﷺ. The revelations he received from God made frequent mention of justice, equity and compassion. It emphasised the importance of socioeconomic justice, brotherhood and freedom. Discussing such lofty social characteristics was, to the hard-hearted Arabs of the sixth century, undoubtedly perilous, given the social and political circumstances. However, the Qur'ānic message was instantly penetrating and persuasive, and it immediately began to supplant the destructive spiritual malaise afflicting those people. In order to eliminate bloodshed and violence, engendered by extreme rancour and hatred, the Prophet ﷺ told the Arabs to purify their hearts of malice and spite, and to enter into the ocean of peace.

Barā' b. ʿĀzib narrates that the Prophet ﷺ said:

---

[1] Qur'ān 17:70.

«أَفْشُوا السَّلَامَ تَسْلَمُوا».

Spread peace, you will be secure.[1]

1.4.1 The Pioneering Nature of the Prophetic Message

Today such rhetoric has become commonplace and thus exhorting such values in the modern context is no great feat. However, in the hostility and turmoil of sixth century Arabia, such words were innovative. Such statements from the Prophet Muhammad ﷺ established a civilisation built on the principles of peace and love. The hadith literature is replete with such sayings from the Messenger of Allah. I will cite a few examples here, to illustrate that love, mercy and peace are the cardinal principles, in which the structure of Islamic civilisation is firmly rooted.

The Prophet ﷺ said to his Companions ﷺ:

«وَالَّذِي نَفْسِي بِيَدِهِ! لَا تَدْخُلُوا الْجَنَّةَ حَتَّى تُؤْمِنُوا، وَلَا تُؤْمِنُوا حَتَّى تَحَابُّوا، أَفَلَا أَدُلُّكُمْ عَلَى أَمْرٍ إِذَا فَعَلْتُمُوهُ تَحَابَبْتُمْ؟ أَفْشُوا السَّلَامَ بَيْنَكُمْ».

By Him in whose hand my life lies, you will never enter paradise until you embrace Islam and you will never become a true Muslim until you love each other. If you want to ask me how to love one another,

---

[1] Related by al-Bukhārī in *al-Adab al-Mufrad*, p. 179 §362; Aḥmad b. Ḥanbal in *al-Musnad*, vol. 4, p. 286 §18557; Ibn Ḥibbān in *al-Ṣaḥīḥ*, vol. 2, pp. 244–245 §491; and Abū Yaʿlā in *al-Musnad*, vol. 2, p. 90 §1687.

> then there is no other way except by spreading peace amongst everybody.[1]

Invoking peace upon fellow Muslims at every meeting is one of the clarion signs of Islam. It serves as a constant reminder to Muslims that the quintessential characteristic of their way of life is peace. Not only will such conduct preserve one's religion, it will also embed in one's heart, love for fellow human beings. The narration succinctly expounds that spreading peace engenders love; love is the basis of faith and only by faith does one enter the Garden.

ʿAbd Allāh b. ʿAmr narrates that the Prophet ﷺ said:

«أُعْبُدُوا الرَّحْمٰنَ، وَأَطْعِمُوا الطَّعَامَ، وَأَفْشُوا السَّلَامَ، تَدْخُلُوا الْجَنَّةَ بِسَلَامٍ».

> Worship the Merciful, feed the hungry, spread peace; you will (as a result) enter Paradise with peace.[2]

In another Prophetic tradition, it is stated:

«إِنَّ السَّلَامَ اسْمٌ مِنْ أَسْمَاءِ اللهِ تَعَالَى، وَضَعَهُ اللهُ فِي الْأَرْضِ، فَأَفْشُوا السَّلَامَ بَيْنَكُمْ».

> Indeed al-Salām is a name of the Names of God, (which) Allah has placed in the earth, so spread peace

---

[1] Related by Abū Dāwūd in *al-Sunan*, vol. 4, p. 389 §5193; Muslim in *al-Ṣaḥīḥ*, vol. 1, p. 74 §54; Ibn Mājah in *al-Sunan*, vol. 1, p. 63 §68 & vol. 2, p. 1217 §3692; and al-Tirmidhī in *al-Sunan*, vol. 5, p. 50 §2688.

[2] Related by al-Tirmidhī in *al-Sunan*, vol. 4, p. 253 §1855; Ibn Mājah in *al-Sunan*, vol. 4, p. 231 §3694; Aḥmad b. Ḥanbal in *al-Musnad*, vol. 2, pp. 170, 196 §6595, 6860; and al-Dārimī in *al-Sunan*, vol. 2, p. 648 §2085.

amongst one another.[1]

In yet another narration, the Prophet ﷺ was asked:

أَيُّ الْإِسْلَامِ خَيْرٌ؟

What Islamic traits are the best?

The Prophet ﷺ replied:

«تُطْعِمُ الطَّعَامَ، وَتَقْرَأُ السَّلَامَ عَلَى مَنْ عَرَفْتَ، وَعَلَى مَنْ لَمْ تَعْرِفْ».

Feed the people, and greet those whom you know and those whom you do not know.[2]

1.5 Examples of Patience, Forbearance, Tolerance and Forgivingness in the Prophet's Character

As stated earlier, there are abundant narrations that illustrate the magnanimity of the Prophetic character, which not only left his Companions in awe of him, but also rendered his enemies speechless.

An example of this is recorded by al-Bukhārī in his collection and is reported by Ibn Abī Mulayka, who said:

عَنْ عَائِشَةَ ﵂: أَنَّ الْيَهُودَ أَتَوُا النَّبِيَّ ﷺ، فَقَالُوا: السَّامُ عَلَيْكَ. قَالَ: «وَعَلَيْكُمْ». فَقَالَتْ عَائِشَةُ: السَّامُ عَلَيْكُمْ، وَلَعَنَكُمُ اللهُ،

---

[1] Related by al-Bukhārī in *al-Adab al-Mufrad*, pp. 182, 201 §372, 426; al-Ṭabarānī in *al-Muʿjam al-Kabīr*, vol. 10, p. 182 §10391; and al-Bayhaqī in *Shuʿab al-Īmān*, vol. 6, p. 433 §8784.

[2] Related by al-Bukhārī in *al-Ṣaḥīḥ*, vol. 5, p. 2302 §5882; and Ibn Manda in *al-Īmān*, vol. 1, p. 453 §357.

وَغَضِبَ عَلَيْكُمْ. فَقَالَ رَسُولُ اللهِ ﷺ: «مَهْلاً يَا عَائِشَةُ! عَلَيْكِ بِالرِّفْقِ، وَإِيَّاكِ وَالْعُنْفَ أَوِ الْفُحْشَ». قَالَتْ: أَوَلَمْ تَسْمَعْ مَا قَالُوا؟ قَالَ: «أَوَلَمْ تَسْمَعِي مَا قُلْتُ؟ رَدَدْتُ عَلَيْهِمْ، فَيُسْتَجَابُ لِي فِيهِمْ، وَلاَ يُسْتَجَابُ لَهُمْ فِيَّ».

ʿĀʾisha ﵂ narrates that: 'Once a group of Jews entered upon the Prophet ﷺ and said: "*al-sāmu ʿalaykum* (death be upon you)." The Prophet ﷺ replied: "The same to you." But ʿĀʾisha ﵂ said: "Death be upon you and the curse and wrath of Allah be upon you." Allah's Messenger ﷺ said: "Calm down, O ʿĀʾisha! You should be lenient and merciful, and must avoid violence and obscenity." She replied: "Haven't you heard what they (the Jews) had said?" Allah's Messenger ﷺ said: "Haven't you heard what I had said (to them)? I have repeated the same words, so my supplication was accepted about them and theirs about me was rejected."'[1]

Another example of the Prophet's tolerance and magnanimity is narrated by the great Successor (*al-tābiʿī*) Mujāhid b. Jubayr, who said: "A goat was slaughtered in the house of ʿAbd Allāh b. ʿUmar. When its meat was served to him, he inquired, 'Have you sent some meat to our Jewish neighbour? I heard the Prophet say: "Jibrīl exhorted me to treat the neighbours well, so much so that I thought he may ask me to make them inheritors."'"[2]

The aforementioned narrations are a mere drop in the ocean of the Prophet's noble character and his sublime

---

[1] Related by al-Bukhārī in *al-Ṣaḥīḥ*, vol. 5, p. 2350 §6038; and *al-Adab al-Mufrad*, pp. 426, 477 §996, 1126.

[2] Related by al-Tirmidhī in *al-Sunan*, vol. 4, p. 294 §1943.

qualities. The reality is that the life of the Prophet ﷺ is inundated with such occurrences and events. These and other such narrations establish beyond a shadow of doubt, that the Prophet ﷺ set a precedent for the greatest ethical, spiritual and sociopolitical revolution in human history. Unfortunately, in our post modern world of confusions and paradoxes, the Prophet Muhammad ﷺ and his enlightening message have been heinously misunderstood in the West and grossly misrepresented by the Muslim world.

There are invaluable lessons in the life of the Prophet ﷺ which provide practical substantiations of the Prophet's chivalrous character. One needs only to look at and contextually understand key points in his blessed life. One such notable occasion is the emigration of the first Muslims from Mecca to Medina. Twelve delegates from Medina, who had come to Mecca during the annual pilgrimage season, pledged their allegiance to the Prophet Muhammad ﷺ and requested the Prophet to migrate to Medina. It is important to note here that before this event, the Prophet Muhammad ﷺ had lived twelve years under the sheer oppression and brutality of the Meccans. He was confined to his house, mocked in the streets of his beloved homeland and stoned by the children of Ṭā'if. However, when the delegates arrived from Medina, pledging their allegiance and absolute obedience to him, he did not narrate to them his story of grief and oppression. Instead he taught them seven basic principles, which, if implemented would initiate an unprecedented spiritual and social reform in the Arabian Peninsula.

He summoned them to faith in the oneness of God. He then ordered them to combat social misdemeanours, prohibiting theft and adultery. He forbade female infanticide, ending centuries of oppression and injustice against women. The Prophet ﷺ prohibited slander, in order to preserve the social repute of every individual, thereby preserving the sanctity of society at large. Finally, the Prophet ﷺ commanded the Medinan delegates to obey him in all the good that he transmits to them.[1]

These seven principles were not only the means of social and political reform, but were also the pivot around which spiritual salvation revolved. As is evident, the primary teachings of the Holy Prophet ﷺ conveyed a sense of tolerance and forgiveness to the Medinans; in an attempt to rid the society of all moral and social ills.

1.6 MIGRATION TO MEDINA

1.6.1 THE FIRST PROPHETIC SERMON IN MEDINA

Similarly, in his first sermon, upon arriving at Medina, the Prophet Muhammad ﷺ summoned the Muslims to adhere to five fundamental teachings. He said:

«أُوصِيكُمْ بِتَقْوَى اللهِ، فَإِنَّهُ خَيْرُ مَا أَوْصَى بِهِ الْـمُسْلِمُ الْـمُسْلِمَ، أَن يَحُضَّهُ عَلَى الآخِرَةِ، وَأَن يَّأْمُرَهُ بِتَقْوَى اللهِ، فَاحْذَرُوْا مَا حَذَّرَكُمُ اللهُ مِنْ نَّفْسِهِ، وَلاَ أَفْضَلَ مِنْ ذَلِكَ نَصِيْحَةً، وَلاَ أَفْضَلَ مِنْ ذَلِكَ ذِكْراً. وَإِنَّهُ تَقْوَى لِمَنْ عَمِلَ بِهِ عَلَى وَجَلٍ وَمَخَافَةٍ مِنْ رَبِّهِ، وَعَوْنِ صِدْقٍ عَلَى مَا تَبْتَغُوْنَ مِنْ أَمْرِ الآخِرَةِ».

I advise you to fear God, for this is the best advice a Muslim can give another Muslim; such that he prompts him about his afterlife and orders him to fear God. Beware of what God has Himself cautioned you. And there is no advice or reminder superior to this. And indeed it is piety for one to accomplish

---

[1] Ibn Hishām, *al-Sīra al-Nabawiyya*, p. 434; Ibn Saʿd, *al-Tabaqāt al-Kubrā*, vol. 1, p. 220; Ibn Kathīr, *al-Bidāya wa al-Nihāya*, vol. 2, p. 526.

this with apprehension and fear of his lord, and is a (means of) true assistance for what desire from the here after.[1]

«أَيُّهَا النَّاسُ! فَقَدِّمُوا لِأَنْفُسِكُمْ، تَعْلُمَنَّ وَاللهِ! لَيُصْعَقَنَّ أَحَدُكُمْ، ثُمَّ لَيَدَعَنَّ غَنَمَهُ لَيْسَ لَهَا رَاعٍ، ثُمَّ لَيَقُولَنَّ لَهُ رَبُّهُ – وَلَيْسَ لَهُ تَرْجُمَانٌ وَلاَ حَاجِبٌ يَحْجِبُهُ دُونَهُ... فَمَا قَدَّمْتَ لِنَفْسِكَ؟ فَلْيَنْظُرَنَّ يَمِينًا وَشِمَالاً فَلاَ يَرَى شَيْئًا، ثُمَّ لَيَنْظُرَنَّ قُدَّامَهُ فَلاَ يَرَى غَيْرَ جَهَنَّمَ».

O mankind! Advance (good deeds) for yourselves! You well know-by Allah-which any one of you may be struck down and thus his flock will be left without a shepherd. Then his Lord will say to him, while he has neither an interpreter nor a veil, to come between them: 'What (good deeds) have you advanced for yourself?' He will look to the right and the left and see nothing. Then he will look before him and only see hell.[2]

«فَمَنِ اسْتَطَاعَ أَن يَقِيَ وَجْهَهُ مِنَ النَّارِ وَلَو بِشِقٍّ تَمْرَةٍ، فَلْيَفْعَلْ. وَمَنْ لَمْ يَجِدْ فَبِكَلِمَةٍ طَيِّبَةٍ، فَإِنَّ بِهَا تُجْزَى الْحَسَنَةُ عَشْرَ أَمْثَالِهَا، إِلَى سَبْعِ مِئَةِ ضِعْفٍ».

So, whoever is able to protect his face from the fire, even by a portion of dates, let him do so. If he finds

[1] Ibn Kathīr, *al-Bidāya wa al-Nihāya*, vol. 2, pp. 603, 604.

[2] Ibn Hishām, *al-Sīra al-Nabawiyya*, p. 496; al-Bayhaqī, *Dalā'il al-Nubuwwa*, vol. 2, p. 524; Ibn Kathīr, *al-Bidāya wa al-Nihāya*, vol. 2, p. 604.

> none then by a kind word for thereby one good deed is rewarded ten times it's like to seven hundred times.[1]

The aforementioned examples eliminate any misunderstanding that the West may have pertaining to the translucent teachings of the Islamic tradition. To bracket violence and brutality with Islam is sheer injustice and is indicative of a deep rooted ignorance of its teachings. From the outset, the Prophet's message was one of love and mercy. He said:

«أَحِبُّوا مَا أَحَبَّ اللهُ، أَحِبُّوا اللهَ مِنْ كُلِّ قُلُوبِكُمْ، وَلاَ تَمَلُّوا كَلاَمَ اللهِ وَذِكْرَهُ، وَلاَ تَقْسُ عَنْهُ قُلُوبُكُمْ».

> Love all that Allah loves. Love Allah with all your heart. Do not tire of His speech and His remembrance and do not harden your hearts (by turning away) from him.[2]

1.6.2 THE FIRST STEP IN THE STATE OF MEDINA: ESTABLISHING INFORMAL SOCIOECONOMIC STABILITY

The Prophet's teachings cultivated a profound sense of mutual love amongst the Muslim community. All his noble statements and actions were redolent of the compassionate teachings of the Islamic tradition. A beautiful illustration of this is when the Prophet Muhammad ﷺ established the pact of brotherhood between the Meccan Emigrants (*al-muhājirūn*) and the

---

[1] Ibn Hishām, *al-Sīra al-Nabawiyya*, p. 496; al-Bayhaqī, *Dalā'il al-Nubuwwa*, vol. 2, p. 524; Ibn Kathīr, *al-Bidāya wa al-Nihāya*, vol. 2, p. 604.

[2] Ibn Hishām, *al-Sīra al-Nabawiyya*, p. 497; al-Bayhaqī, *Dalā'il al-Nubuwwa*, vol. 2, p. 525; Ibn Kathīr, *al-Bidāya wa al-Nihāya*, vol. 2, p. 605.

Medinan Helpers (*al-anṣār*). The Holy Prophet's first step in establishing the state of Medina was not to enforce the laws of worship or institute the penal system. Rather the Prophet's priority was to establish social equilibrium, beginning with the just distribution of wealth. The act of brotherhood thus formed unwavering bonds of love and compassion between the citizens of the Medinan state, as well as engendering socioeconomic stability for the Muslim.

1.6.3 The First Constitution in Human History: The Constitution of Medina

The second most significant step the Prophet ﷺ took upon arriving in Medina was to form a political alliance with the Jews, Christians and other non-Muslim minorities residing in Medina. A formal agreement was drafted, aimed at bringing an end to the bitter cycles of violence between the conflicting clans of Medina. The document, famously known as the Constitution of Medina, became the first written constitution in human history. In order to understand the significance of this constitution, let us take a cursory look at the development of constitutional history.

1.7 Constitutional History: A Comparative Glance

1.7.1 The British Constitution

It is well documented that British constitutional history begins in 1100 AD with the Charter of Liberties. In 1215 King John I signed the Magna Carta, which became the first constitutional document in British history. Britain became a constitutional state with the signing of the Magna Carta and 474 years later, in 1689, the Bill of Rights was prepared. In 1701 the act of

Settlement was passed followed by the Parliament Act in 1911.[1]

1.7.2 THE US CONSTITUTION

In 1787 America declared its separation from Britain, before which Thomas Jefferson gave the declaration of Independence in July 1776. A constitutional convention took place in 1780 followed by the Philadelphia Convention of 1787. Then the Great Compromise of American history takes place, and on the 17th of September 1787, a constitutional convention finally approved a constitution for the US. In 1865, through the 13th amendment, they approved human rights as part of the American constitution. Then in 1920, less than a 100 years ago, through the 19th amendment, gender discrimination was removed from the constitution and women were granted the right to vote.[2]

1.7.3 THE MEDINAN CONSTITUTION

This brief overview of constitutional development in the West allows us to compare it with constitutional development in the Islamic world. Issues that were settled in the West no more than a hundred years ago were well documented in the constitution of Islam by the Prophet of Islam ﷺ fourteen centuries ago. In his constitution, the Prophet Muhammad ﷺ addressed his

[1] Knappen, M. M., Constitutional and Legal History of England, New York: Harcourt Brace, 1942; J. E. A. Jolliffe, The Constitutional History of Medieval England from the English Settlement to 1485, D. Van Nostrand Company, Inc., New York; Selected Documents of English Constitutional History, Ed. By George Burton Adams & H. Morse Stephens, London: Macmillan & Co., Ltd. 1901.

[2] Hart, James, The American Presidency in Action 1789: A Study in Constitutional History, New York, The Macmillan Company, 1948; Melvin I. Urofsky, Paul Finkelman, A March of Liberty: A Constitutional History of the United States (two volumes), Oxford University Press, 2002.

community thus:

«هَذَا كِتَابٌ مِنْ مُحَمَّدٍ النَّبِيِّ الأُمِّيِّ بَيْنَ الْـمُؤْمِنِيْنَ وَالْـمُسْلِمِيْنَ مِنْ قُرَيْشٍ، وَيَثْرِبَ وَمَنْ تَبِعَهُمْ، فَلَحِقَ بِهِمْ وَجَاهَدَ مَعَهُمْ أَنَّهُمْ أُمَّةٌ وَّاحِدَةٌ مِّنْ دُوْنِ النَّاسِ».

> This is a constitutional document from Muhammad, the *Ummī* Prophet, to all the believers and Muslims from Quraysh (who have emigrated) and Yathrib, and those (non-Muslim tribes) who follow them, joined them and will fight with them. They are all (henceforth) one community, besides the rest of mankind.[1]

A complete structure of governance was established on the basis of this constitution. Governors were appointed and power was delegated at the provincial level, forming a local government system for the first time in Medina. Political unity was created in the form of a nation-state and the Holy Prophet ﷺ enforced a system based on the rule of law. One must keep in mind that this was a time when the mere word of the ruler was the law. There was no sophisticated methodology by which laws were deduced and instituted. Concepts such as consultative law, mutual assemblies, and passing resolutions (prior to the enforcement of a law) were all unheard of. These and many other political concepts were introduced to the Arabs, and by extension to the world, by the Universal Prophet ﷺ.

---

[1] Ibn Kathīr, *al-Bidāya wa al-Nihāya*, vol. 2, p. 620; and Abū ʿUbayd al-Qāsim b. al-Sallām, *Kitāb al-Amwāl*, p. 194 §518.

1.7.3.1 Religious Freedom and the Historic Condemnation of Terrorism and Acts of Violence against Non-Muslims

For the first time in history a constitution declared that Muslims must coexist with non-Muslim tribes in the spirit of conviviality and mutual respect. The constitution of Medina did not sanctify war against the Jews, Christians or any other non-Muslim tribes. In fact the non-Muslim minorities were under a covenant of protection and security, such that they were allowed to retain their local customs and religious practices, without facing antagonist reactions from the Muslims. Such actions initiated the development of a United Arabia under the banner of Islam. All this was possible as a direct result of the social and political reform instigated through the Constitution of Medina. Article sixteen of the Charter states:

«وَإِنَّ الْـمُؤْمِنِيْنَ الْـمُتَّقِيْنَ أَيْدِيهِمْ عَلَى كُلِّ مَنْ بَغَى وَابْتَغَى مِنْهُمْ دَسِيْعَةَ ظُلْمٍ أَوْ إِثْمٍ، أَوْ عُدْوَانٍ أَوْ فَسَادٍ بَيْنَ الْـمُؤْمِنِيْنَ، وَأَنَّ أَيْدِيَهُم عَلَيْهِ جَمِيعًا وَلَوْ كَانَ وَلَدَ أَحَدِهِمْ».

> There shall be collective resistance by the believers against any individual who rises in rebellion, attempts to acquire anything by force, violates any pledge or attempts to spread mischief amongst the believers. Such collective resistance against the perpetrator shall occur even if he is the son of anyone of them.[1]

Hence any act of terrorism or violence under the constitution would amount to a crime and was accordingly punished. The charter not only guaranteed freedom to practice religion and prohibited acts of violence, it also placed responsibility on

[1] Abū ʿUbayd al-Qāsim b. al-Sallām, *Kitāb al-Amwāl*, p. 194 §518.

the citizens of Medina, be they Muslims or non-Muslims, to collectively resist such acts.

Contrary to prevalent misconceptions in the West, Islam is neither an intrinsically violent religion, nor does it endorse a violent agenda. Even the most cursory perusal of early Islamic history, specifically the Prophetic period, provide ample insight into the merciful nature of Islam, in its most pure and unadulterated form. Unfortunately, certain zealots amongst the Muslim community, due to their ignorance of the primary sources of the Islamic tradition, present a narrow and utterly contorted image of this sophisticated tradition. The likes of Osama Bin Laden, are neither the scholars of Islam, nor are they its true representatives; and hence they bear no authority to declare jihad on behalf of the Muslims. It is the duty of the majority of Muslims to shun such despotic views and proffer the true understanding of Islam, which is anchored in 1400 years of scrupulous scholarship and meticulous transmission.

1.8 Women's Rights: A Comparative Overview

1.8.1 Taliban do not Represent an Islamic Government

In addition to what has been stated thus far, another noteworthy achievement of Islam is the freedom of women. Due to the lack of access to the original sources of Islamic Law, many estranged minds assume that Islam discriminates against women. Unfortunately, misrepresentation by self-proclaimed 'Islamic' governments, such as the Taliban, has unequivocally increased the misgivings. However, the reality is that neither the Taliban, nor any other 'pseudo-Islamic' systems for that matter, comply with the Prophetic model, implemented in the state of Medina.

1.8.2 Women's Rights in the West

I will again provide a brief overview of the development of women's rights and the elimination of gender discrimination in the West vis-à-vis the Prophetic model. As a matter of historical fact, in the Western world, a woman was not even considered a 'legal person' until early 20th century.

Rogger Cotterrel proffers a definition of a legal person, in his work, *The Sociology of Law*, stating, "a legal person or legal subject defines who or what the law will recognise as a being capable of having rights and duties, the one who possess legal rights and duties is known to be the legal person."[1]

1.8.2.1 Development of Women's Rights in Britain

In Britain, women began their political and social struggle to attain recognition as legal personnel and to attain the right to vote in 1897, with the formation of the National Union of Women's Suffrage by Millicent Fawlett. This Union was further strengthened by the Women's Social and Political Union, established in 1903. In 1918, after immense struggle, the Representation of People Act sanctioned women over the age of 30 to vote.[2] However, this in no way eliminated gender-based discrimination, since men were allowed to vote at 21 and those in the army even younger, at 19.

1.8.2.2 Development of Women's Rights in the US

A similar account of discrimination and subsequent struggle is

---

1 Cotterrell, Roger, *The Sociology of Law*, pp. 123–124.

2 *Electioneering: A Comparative Study of Continuity and Change*, Ed. by David Butler and Austin Ranney, Oxford: Clarendon Press, 1992, p. 64.

found in the United States of America.

The 1776 US Declaration of Independence makes no reference at all to women's rights. In fact Richard Nelson remarks that, "in colonial society a married woman had virtually no rights, the revolution did nothing to change this."[1] The same view is echoed by James Burns who asserts that the declaration refers to men, not women.[2]

The discrimination against women, was of such intensity that in 1872, Susan Anthony, the champion of women's rights activism in the US, was jailed for casting a vote in the presidential elections; since being a woman, she had no legal right to do so. It was only as late as 1919 that discrimination on the basis of gender was *de jure* abolished, through the 19th constitutional amendment.

1.8.2.3 DEVELOPMENT OF WOMEN'S RIGHTS IN FRANCE

A similar paradigm is found in France; where, although democracy was declared in 1848, women were not allowed to vote until as late as 1944, after almost a century of suppression and struggle.

1.8.2.4 WOMEN'S RIGHT TO VOTE IN VARIOUS OTHER COUNTRIES

In Australia women attained the right to vote in 1921; the first lady was elected through this vote. In New Zealand, women got the right to vote in 1893; in Finland it was in 1906, Norway in 1907, Denmark in 1915, Germany in 1918, Austria

---

[1] Alan Brinkley, Frank Freidel, Richard Nelson Current, Harry T. Williams, *American History: A Survey*, Edition 7, New York, 1987, p. 122.

[2] Jefferson, *Government by the People*, edition 15, Prentice Hall, 1993, p. 117.

in 1919, Canada in 1919, Netherlands in 1919, Belgium in 1919, Switzerland in 1971, Ireland in 1918, Luxemburg in 1919, Spain in 1931, Poland in 1918, and Brazil in 1937.

The above presented examples are paradigmatic of the entire Western World. In general, women were neither recognised as legal subjects nor granted the right to vote until the late 19th or early 20th century and history is very clear about that.

1.8.3 Women's Rights in Islamic Law Fourteen Centuries Ago

Interestingly, women were declared legal personnel in Islamic Law over fourteen centuries ago. They were given the right to vote and to partake in the political process of the day.

The Qur'ān states:

﴿يَٰٓأَيُّهَا ٱلنَّبِيُّ إِذَا جَآءَكَ ٱلْمُؤْمِنَٰتُ يُبَايِعْنَكَ عَلَىٰٓ أَن لَّا يُشْرِكْنَ
بِٱللَّهِ شَيْـًٔا وَلَا يَسْرِقْنَ وَلَا يَزْنِينَ وَلَا يَقْتُلْنَ أَوْلَٰدَهُنَّ وَلَا يَأْتِينَ
بِبُهْتَٰنٍ يَفْتَرِينَهُۥ بَيْنَ أَيْدِيهِنَّ وَأَرْجُلِهِنَّ وَلَا يَعْصِينَكَ فِى
مَعْرُوفٍ فَبَايِعْهُنَّ وَٱسْتَغْفِرْ لَهُنَّ ٱللَّهَ ۖ إِنَّ ٱللَّهَ غَفُورٌ رَّحِيمٌ﴾

O Prophet! When the believing women appear in your presence to take the oath of allegiance that they will not set up anything as partner with Allah and will not steal, nor will they commit adultery or kill their children or bring false blame which they have invented between their hands and feet (i.e. will not deceive their husbands declaring someone else's baby as born to her) or disobey you in what is right, then accept their allegiance and seek forgiveness for them from Allah. Surely Allah is Most Forgiving, Ever Merciful.[1]

---

[1] Qur'ān 60: 12.

While developing the structure of the Islamic state, several ladies were brought in as active participants in the state apparatus. Women were appointed as members of parliament, officers, and administrators in the administrative structure of the state of Medina.

1.8.4 MUSLIM WOMEN HELD PROMINENT ROLES IN EARLY ISLAMIC HISTORY

One such example is that of Shifāʾ bint ʿAbd Allāh al-ʿAdawiyya who was appointed as a judge of the accountability court and market administrator in the reign of the second rightly-guided caliph ʿUmar b. al-Khaṭṭāb ﵁.[1] Ladies were appointed as ambassadors and as diplomats. In the tenure of the third rightly-guided caliph ʿUthmān ﵁, Umm Kulthūm, daughter of ʿAlī b. Abī Ṭālib ﵄ was sent in 28th AH as an ambassador to the Queen of the Roman Empire.[2] Women were given offices and responsibilities in the military services. Imam al-Bukhārī reports a narration of Anas b. Mālik ﵁ about ʿĀʾisha ﵂ and Umm Sulaym ﵂ performing duties in the battle of Uḥud, in the lifetime of the Prophet ﷺ himself.[3] Many other women worked as military officers in military expeditions.

Some narrations, pertinent to our disquisitions are presented below:

عَنْ أَنَسٍ ﵁ يَقُولُ: دَخَلَ رَسُولُ اللهِ ﷺ عَلَى ابْنَةِ مِلْحَانَ، فَاتَّكَأَ
عِنْدَهَا، ثُمَّ ضَحِكَ، فَقَالَتْ: لِمَ تَضْحَكُ يَا رَسُولَ اللهِ؟ فَقَالَ:
«نَاسٌ مِنْ أُمَّتِي يَرْكَبُونَ الْبَحْرَ الْأَخْضَرَ فِي سَبِيلِ اللهِ مَثَلُهُمْ مَثَلُ

[1] Ibn azm, *al-Muḥallā*, vol. 9, p. 429; Ibn ʿAbd al-Barr, *al-Iistīʿāb*, vol. 4, p. 341.

[2] Ibn Jarīr al-Ṭabarī, *Tārīkh al-Umam wa al-Mulūk*, vol. 2, p. 601.

[3] Related by al-Bukhārī in *al-Ṣaḥīḥ*, vol. 3, pp. 1055, 1056 §2724.

الْـمُلُوكِ عَلَى الْأَسِرَّةِ». فَقَالَتْ: يَا رَسُولَ اللهِ! ادْعُ اللهَ أَنْ يَجْعَلَنِي مِنْهُمْ. قَالَ: «اللَّهُمَّ اجْعَلْهَا مِنْهُمْ». ثُمَّ عَادَ، فَضَحِكَ، فَقَالَتْ لَهُ مِثْلَ، أَوْ مِمَّ ذَلِكَ. فَقَالَ لَهَا مِثْلَ ذَلِكَ، فَقَالَتْ: ادْعُ اللهَ أَنْ يَجْعَلَنِي مِنْهُمْ. قَالَ: «أَنْتِ مِنَ الْأَوَّلِينَ، وَلَسْتِ مِنَ الْآخِرِينَ». قَالَ: قَالَ أَنَسٌ: فَتَزَوَّجَتْ عُبَادَةَ بْنَ الصَّامِتِ، فَرَكِبَتِ الْبَحْرَ مَعَ بِنْتِ قَرَظَةَ، فَلَمَّا قَفَلَتْ، رَكِبَتْ دَابَّتَهَا، فَوَقَصَتْ بِهَا، فَسَقَطَتْ عَنْهَا فَمَاتَتْ.

According to Anas b. Mālik ﵁: 'Allah's Messenger ﷺ went to the daughter of Milḥān and reclined there (and slept) and then (woke up) smiling. She asked: "O Allah's Messenger! What makes you smile?" He replied: "(I dreamt that) some people amongst my followers were sailing on the green sea in Allah's Cause, resembling kings on thrones." She said: "O Allah's Messenger! Invoke Allah to make me one of them." He said: "O Allah! Let her be one of them." Then he (slept again and woke up and) smiled. She asked him the same question and he gave the same reply. She said: "Invoke Allah to make me one of them." He replied: "You will be amongst the first group of them; you will not be amongst the last." Later, she married ʿUbāda b. al-Ṣmit ﵁ and then she sailed on the sea with Bint Qaraẓa, Muʿāwiyya's wife. On her return, she mounted her riding animal, which threw her down breaking her neck, and she died on falling down.'[1]

[1] Related by al-Bukhārī in *al-Ṣaḥīḥ*, vol. 3, p. 1055 §2722.

Tha'laba b. Mālik ؓ reported:

إِنَّ عُمَرَ بْنَ الْخَطَّابِ ؓ قَسَمَ مُرُوطًا بَيْنَ نِسَاءٍ مِنْ نِسَاءِ الْمَدِينَةِ، فَبَقِيَ مِرْطٌ جَيِّدٌ، فَقَالَ لَهُ بَعْضُ مَنْ عِنْدَهُ: يَا أَمِيرَ الْمُؤْمِنِينَ! أَعْطِ هَذَا ابْنَةَ رَسُولِ اللهِ ﷺ الَّتِي عِنْدَكَ - يُرِيدُونَ أُمَّ كُلْثُومٍ بِنْتَ عَلِيٍّ - فَقَالَ عُمَرُ: أُمُّ سَلِيطٍ أَحَقُّ، وَأُمُّ سَلِيطٍ مِنْ نِسَاءِ الْأَنْصَارِ مِمَّنْ بَايَعَ رَسُولَ اللهِ ﷺ. قَالَ عُمَرُ: فَإِنَّهَا كَانَتْ تَزْفِرُ لَنَا الْقِرَبَ يَوْمَ أُحُدٍ.

'Umar b. al-Khaṭṭāb ؓ distributed some garments amongst the women of Medina. One garment remained, and one of those present with him said: 'O leader of the faithful! Give this garment to your wife, the (grand) daughter of Allah's Messenger ﷺ.' They meant Umm Kulthūm, the daughter of 'Alī ؓ. 'Umar ؓ said: 'Umm Salīṭ ؓ has more right (to have it). Umm Salīṭ ؓ was amongst those women of Medinan Helpers who had given the pledge of allegiance to Allah's Messenger ﷺ.' 'Umar ؓ said: 'She (ie Umm Salīṭ) used to carry the water skins for us on the day of Uḥud.'[1]

It has been narrated on the authority of Umm 'Aṭiyya, the Ansarite ؓ:

غَزَوْتُ مَعَ رَسُولِ اللهِ ﷺ سَبْعَ غَزَوَاتٍ، أَخْلُفُهُمْ فِي رِحَالِهِمْ، فَأَصْنَعُ لَهُمُ الطَّعَامَ، وَأُدَاوِي الْجَرْحَى، وَأَقُومُ عَلَى الْمَرْضَى.

I took part with the Messenger of Allah ﷺ in seven battles. I would stay behind in the camp of men, cook

---

[1] Related by al-Bukhārī in *al-Ṣaḥīḥ*, vol. 3, p. 1056 §2725.

their food, treat the wounded and nurse the sick.[1]

Anas b. Mālik ﷺ narrated:

كَانَ رَسُولُ اللهِ ﷺ يَغْزُو بِأُمِّ سُلَيْمٍ وَنِسْوَةٍ مِنَ الْأَنْصَارِ، لِيَسْقِينَ الْمَاءَ وَيُدَاوِينَ الْجَرْحَى.

Allah's Messenger ﷺ went on an expedition; he took Umm Sulaym and some Ansarite women who supplied water and tended the wounded.[2]

The legal status of women was unequivocally protected in the blessed epoch of the Prophet ﷺ such that if a women provided legal protection to anyone in her house, the state was obliged to respect the commitment. Zaynab ﷺ granted protection to her husband, Abū al-ʿĀṣ and the state accepted this.[3] Abū Hurayra ﷺ narrated that the Holy Prophet ﷺ said:

«إِنَّ الْمَرْأَةَ لَتَأْخُذُ لِلْقَوْمِ يَعْنِي تُجِيرُ عَلَى الْمُسْلِمِينَ».

Verily, woman can give legal protection to the whole community and that would be considered valid by the state.[4]

Another narration is reported as follows:

«إِنْ كَانَتِ الْمَرْأَةُ لَتُجِيرُ عَلَى الْمُؤْمِنِيْنَ فَيَجُوْزُ».

If a woman would give security from the believers, it

---

[1] Related by Muslim in *al-Ṣaḥīḥ*, vol. 3, p. 1447 §1812.

[2] Related by Abū Dāwūd in *al-Sunan*, vol. 2, p. 357 §2531; al-Tirmidhī in *al-Sunan*, vol. 4, p. 118 §1575; and Ibn Ḥibbān in *al-Ṣaḥīḥ*, vol. 11, p. 26 §4723.

[3] Ibn Hishām, *al-Sīra al-Nabawiyya*, pp. 636–638.

[4] Related by al-Tirmidhī in *al-Sunan*, vol. 4, p. 120 §1579.

would be valid.[1]

In general, women were pivotal contributors to the formation of the Islamic society. One of the most effective roles women fulfilled was in parliament, where female members spoke eloquently about issues confronting women specifically. A powerful illustration of this in political discourse is when ʿUmar wished to pass a bill, to limit the amount of dowry that could be paid to a women. A female member of the parliament voiced her disagreement exclaiming, 'do you wish to limit the dowry O ʿUmar, when Allah has not.' ʿUmar requested evidence and she responded with a verse of the Qurʾān, which states,

﴿وَإِنْ أَرَدتُّمُ ٱسْتِبْدَالَ زَوْجٍ مَّكَانَ زَوْجٍ وَءَاتَيْتُمْ إِحْدَىٰهُنَّ قِنطَارًا فَلَا تَأْخُذُوا۟ مِنْهُ شَيْـًٔا أَتَأْخُذُونَهُۥ بُهْتَـٰنًا وَإِثْمًا مُّبِينًا﴾

⁂And if you seek to take a wife in place of another and you have given to one of them heaps of wealth, take (back) nothing of it. Do you take it (the wealth back) by means of calumny and manifest sin.⁂[2]

ʿUmar instantly changed his views and proclaimed that "the woman was right and the man wrong."[3]

There are abundant historical examples of this nature, which give us an insight into the political, social and legal status enjoyed by the female citizens of the Medinan state. On the contrary such rights were accorded to women in the West merely a hundred years ago, after decades of relentless struggles and suffering.

---

[1] Related by Abū Dāwūd in *al-Sunan*, vol. 3, p. 422 §2764.

[2] Qurʾān 4:20.

[3] ʿAbd al-Razzāq, *al-Muṣannaf*, vol. 6, p. 180 §10420; al-Shawkānī, *Nayl al-Awṭār*, vol. 6, p. 314.

One of the greatest examples of intellectual freedom enjoyed by Muslim women is that of Lady ʿĀʾisha رضي الله عنها, the noble wife of the Prophet ﷺ. Lady ʿĀʾisha was a true polymath; for not only was she an exemplary hadith master, she was also a specialist in jurisprudence, history, literature and astronomy.

Lady Sukayna, daughter of usayn b. ʿAlī رضي الله عنه, was also an expert in literature and poetry. amrāʾ bint Ziyādat, ʿĀʾisha al-Bāʿūniyya and Maymūna bint Saʿd were experts on poetry, literature and various fields of knowledge. Sayyida Shahīda, who died five years after the migration to Medina was an expert in literature and history. Fātima bint ʿAlī b. Husayn was an expert in the anbalī legal tradition and numerous Islamic scholars received knowledge from her. asan al-Baṣrī received knowledge from Rābiʿa al-Qasīsa. Sharīfa Fāṭima was the governor of Yemen, Ṣanʿāʾ and Najrān. Shifāʾ bint ʿAbd Allāh Makhzūmiyya was a judge of the court in the days of ʿUmar رضي الله عنه. Ḥanīfa Khānūn, the niece of Sulṭān Ṣalāḥ al-Dīn al-Ayyūbī, was the governor of Ḥalab.

A detailed study of the great women who played central roles in erecting the edifice of the Islamic legal, political and spiritual edifice is outside of the scope of our disquisitions here and would require volumes.

1.9 MUSLIM AND NON-MUSLIM RELATIONS

An issue severely misunderstood in modern times is the relationship between Muslims and non-Muslims. During early Muslim rule the non-Muslims constituted a minority and Muslims were the rulers.

It is narrated that the Prophet ﷺ said:

«أَلَا! مَنْ ظَلَمَ مُعَاهِدًا أَوْ انْتَقَصَهُ أَوْ كَلَّفَهُ فَوْقَ طَاقَتِهِ، أَوْ أَخَذَ مِنْهُ شَيْئًا بِغَيْرِ طِيبِ نَفْسٍ، فَأَنَا حَجِيجُهُ يَوْمَ الْقِيَامَةِ».

Beware, if anyone wrongs someone in (a legal)

> contract (i.e. minorities) or diminishes his right, or burdens him (to work) beyond his capacity, or takes from him anything without his consent, I shall plead for him (against the Muslim) on the Day of Judgment.[1]

1.9.1 CAPITAL PUNISHMENT AWARDED TO A MUSLIM FOR MURDERING A NON-MUSLIM

ʿAbd al-Raḥmān b. Baylamānī ﷺ states:

أَنَّ رَجُـلًا مِنَ الْـمُسْلِمِيْنَ قَتَلَ رَجُلًا مِنْ أَهْلِ الْكِتَابِ، فَرُفِعَ إِلَى النَّبِيِّ ﷺ، فَقَالَ رَسُوْلُ اللهِ ﷺ: «أَنَا أَحَقُّ مَنْ وَفَى بِذِمَّتِهِ»، ثُمَّ أَمَرَ بِهِ فَقُتِلَ.

> On one occasion a Muslim killed one of the People of the Book (a man who was either a Jew or a Christian). The case was referred to the Prophet Muhammad ﷺ. Allah's Messenger ﷺ said: 'I am most responsible to fulfil the rights of minorities.' Then he ordered the capital punishment against the Muslim and he was killed.[2]

Thus the Holy Prophet ﷺ declared that the blood of a Muslim and a non-Muslim had equal status.

1.9.2 THE PROPHET ﷺ HONOURED HIS CHRISTIAN GUESTS

An example that illustrates the Prophet's kindness towards

[1] Related by Abū Dāwūd in *al-Sunan*, vol. 3, p. 108 §3052.

[2] Set forth by al-Shāfiʿī in *al-Musnad*, pp. 343, 344 and *al-Umm*, vol. 7, p. 320; Abū Nuʿaym in *Musnad Abī Ḥanīfa*, p. 104; al-Shaybānī in *al-Mabsūṭ*, vol. 4, p. 488; al-Bayhaqī in *al-Sunan al-Kubrā*, vol. 8, p. 30 §15696.

non-Muslim was on the occasion when a delegate of Christians from Negus[1] visited Allah's Messenger ﷺ, and he arose to serve them. His Companions ؓ requested: "let us do that for you, O Allah's Messenger." He replied: "they honoured my Companions, and I wish to pay them back."[2]

On another occasion the Holy Prophet ﷺ allowed a delegate of Christians from Najrān to reside in his Mosque. When the time came for them to worship, they asked for permission, and the Holy Prophet allowed them to worship according to their own religion in the Mosque.[3] Such was the level of religious freedom granted to non-Muslims by the Prophet Muhammad ﷺ.

1.9.3 Forgiveness of the Former Oppressors of Muslims at the Bloodless Conquest of Mecca

Consider for a moment the time of the conquest of Mecca when the Prophet ﷺ entered the Sacred City as a conqueror with an army of 10,000 men. The Meccans surrendered willingly and there was no bloodshed. However had the Prophet ﷺ intended he could have sought revenge for the suffering he had endured at their hands. He and the early Muslims not only suffered prosecution and humiliation but several attempts were also made to assassinate him. It was in such dire circumstances that the Prophet ﷺ had been forced to leave his beloved city. Upon entering Mecca one Ansarite commander Saʿd b. ʿUbāda ؓ declared passionately: 'Today is the day of war.' The Holy Prophet ﷺ expressed displeasure at this statement, took the

---

[1] Negus was the then king of Abyssinia.
[2] Related by al-Bayhaqī in *Shuʿab al-Īmān*, vol. 6, p. 518 §9125; and b. Kathīr in *al-Bidāya wa al-Nihāya*, vol. 2, p. 431.
[3] Related by Ibn Saʿd in *al-Ṭabaqāt al-Kubrā*, vol. 1, p. 357; and b. al-Qayyim in *Zād al-Maʿād*, vol. 3, p. 629.

flag from him and handed it over to his son and said to Abū Sufyān:

$$\text{اَلْيَوْمُ يَوْمُ الْـمَرْحَمَةِ.}$$

Today is the day of mercy.[1]

Then the Holy Prophet ﷺ asked his enemies: "What kind of behaviour do you expect from me today?" They replied: "We expect the same behaviour as the one Prophet Yūsuf ؑ extended to his brothers." The Holy Prophet ﷺ said what Prophet Yūsuf ؑ had announced:

$$\text{«اذْهَبُوا فَأَنْتُمُ الطُّلَقَاءُ».}$$

Go, for you are free (of all blame and punishment).[2]

This is one of the many examples illustrating the magnanimity of the Prophet Muhammad ﷺ. At that time one of his greatest opponents were Abū Sufyān and the two sons of Abū Lahab. However, after the conquest, the Prophet Muhammad ﷺ declared the house of Abū Sufyān secure such that whosoever entered it would be protected.[3] The sons of Abū Lahab, a vehement enemy of Islam, feared being killed so they hid under the covering of the ka'ba but when the Holy Prophet ﷺ found them he forgave them.[4] Through such gracious conduct the Prophet Muhammad ﷺ single-handedly united Arabia and left behind for his followers a legacy of love, compassion and tolerance.

---

[1] Related by Ibn Ḥajar al-'Asqalānī in *Fatḥ al-Bārī*, vol. 8, pp. 8–9; and b. 'Abd al-Barr in *al-Istī'āb*, vol. 2, p. 163.

[2] Related by Ibn Ḥajar al-'Asqalānī in *Fatḥ al-Bārī*, vol. 8, pp. 18, 19.

[3] Related by Muslim in *al-Ṣaḥīḥ*, vol. 3, pp. 1405–1408 §1780; Abū Dāwūd in *al-Sunan*, vol. 3, p. 197 §3021; and al-Dāraquṭnī in *al-Sunan*, vol. 3, p. 60 §233.

[4] Related by al-Zayla'ī in *Naṣb al-Rāya*, vol. 3, p. 336.

Those who claim that Islam was spread by the sword and that it advocates perpetual warfare, need only to sincerely study the life of the Prophet ﷺ and early Islamic history. One will undoubtedly find that the Prophet ﷺ never initiated a war against the Meccans. In fact, both the battles of Badr and Uḥud were fought on the borders of Medina and the Prophet ﷺ was defending his city. Aggression and violence were not part of his noble nature and his life and teachings are a testimony to that. Human history has never witnessed an individual as wholly and utterly devoted to the principles of peace like the Prophet ﷺ.

1.9.4 ISLAMIC LAW PRESCRIBES JUSTICE AND EQUITY FOR NON-MUSLIMS

Books of Prophetic traditions are replete with noble sayings, which expound the loftiest ethical principles humankind ever knew. The Prophet ﷺ was a fount of justice, love and mercy. His character epitomised human dignity. He ﷺ said,

«أَنَا أَحَقُّ مَنْ وَفَى بِذِمَّتِهِ».

> I am the most worthy of those who fulfill their responsibility (i.e. with regards to non-Muslims).[1]

ʿAlī b. Abī Ṭālib رضي الله عنه said:

«إِذَا قَتَلَ الْـمُسْلِمُ النَّصْرَانِيَّ قُتِلَ بِهِ».

> If a Muslim kills a Christian, he will be killed (in retaliation).[2]

---

[1] Set forth by al-Shāfiʿī in *al-Musnad*, pp. 343, 344 and *al-Umm*, vol. 7, p. 320; Abū Nuʿaym in *Musnad Abī Ḥanīfa*, p. 104; al-Shaybānī in *al-Mabsūṭ*, vol. 4, p. 488; al-Bayhaqī in *al-Sunan al-Kubrā*, vol. 8, p. 30 §15696.

[2] Related by al-Shaybānī in *al- ujja*, vol. 4, p. 349; al-Shāfiʿī in *al-*

1.9.5 THE BLOOD MONEY (*DIYYA*) OF A NON-MUSLIM IS EQUAL TO THAT OF A MUSLIM

Imam Abū Ḥanīfa said:

$$\text{دِيَةُ الْيَهُوْدِيِّ وَالنَّصْرَانِيِّ وَالْـمَجُوْسِيِّ مِثْلُ دِيَةِ الْحُرِّ الْـمُسْلِمِ.}$$

The blood-money of a Jew, Christian and Zoroastrian is equal to that of a free Muslim.[1]

ʿAmr b. al-ʿĀṣ was the Governor of Egypt and his son gave an illegal punishment to a non-Muslim. The case was referred to ʿUmar, who gave punishment to the son of ʿAmr b. al-ʿĀṣ openly and said to him:

$$\text{مُذْ كَمِ اسْتَعْبَدْتُمُ النَّاسَ وَقَدْ وَلَدَتْهُمْ أُمَّهَاتُهُمْ أَحْرَارًا؟}$$

Since when have you made people your slaves when their mother gave birth to them as free men?[2]

Renowned hadith-scholar Ibn Shihāb al-Zuhrī states that during the caliphate of Abū Bakr, ʿUmar and ʿUthmān the blood money of the non-Muslim citizens of the Islamic state was equal to that of Muslims.[3]

It is mentioned by Ibn Saʿd in *al-Ṭabaqāt al-Kubrā* (vol. 1, p. 358) that the Holy Prophet wrote a letter to the people of Najrān when they had announced their affiliation to the Islamic state of Medina. That letter says:

Umm, vol. 7, p. 320; and al-Shawkānī in *Nayl al-Awṭār*, vol. 7, p. 154.

[1] Related by Ibn Abī Shayba in *al-Muṣannaf*, vol. 5, p. 407 §27448; ʿAbd al-Razzāq in *al-Muṣannaf*, vol. 10, pp. 95, 97, 99; al-Shaybānī in *al-Ḥujja*, vol. 4, pp. 322, 323; and al-Shawkānī in *Nayl al-Awṭār*, vol. 7, p. 154.

[2] Related by al-Hindī in *Kanz al-ʿUmmāl*, vol. 12, pp. 660, 661 §36010.

[3] Related by al-Shaybānī in *al-Ḥujja*, vol. 4, p. 351; and al-Shawkānī in *Nayl al-Awṭār*, vol. 7, p. 321.

«لِنَجْرَانَ وَحَاشِيَتِهِمْ جِوَارُ اللهِ وَذِمَّةُ مُحَمَّدٍ النَّبِيِّ رَسُوْلِ اللهِ ﷺ عَلَى أَنْفُسِهِمْ وَمِلَّتِهِمْ وَأَرْضِهِمْ وَأَمْوَالِهِمْ وَغَائِبِهِمْ وَشَاهِدِهِمْ وَبِيَعِهِمْ، لاَ يُغَيَّرُوا أُسْقُفُ عَنْ سَقِيْفَاهُ، وَلاَ رَاهِبُ عَنْ رَهْبَانِيَّتِهِ، وَلاَ وَاقِفٌ عَنْ وَقْفَانِيَّتِهِ».

Najrān and its allies (who have accepted the authority of the State of Medina) have the guaranteed protection of Allah and the Prophet Muhammad, Allah's Messenger; (this protection extends) to their lives, religion, land, wealth; to all those who are present or absent as well as their business. (It is also my order for the Muslim government that) no priest, monk or chief is removed from his office.

1.9.6 Social Benefits and Income Support for Jobless, Old, or Disabled Non-Muslims Living in an Islamic State

The Prophet ﷺ and the Rightly Guided Caliphs declared that the non-Muslims in the Islamic state would be entitled to all social benefits that the Muslims were entitled to. Assistance was provided for elderly and ill non-Muslims as it was provided for the Muslims. It is reported by Saʿīd b. al-Musayyab that the Prophet ﷺ gave charity to a Jewish household and this practice continued after his demise.[1]

ʿAmr b. Maymūn, ʿAmr b. Sharjīl and Murra Hamdhānī stated that they used to give a portion of charity of *fiṭr* to Christian monks.[2]

Imam Yūsuf stated: "If non-Muslim citizens of the Islamic

---

[1] Abū ʿUbayd al-Qāsim b. al-Sallām, *Kitāb al-Amwāl*, p. 543 §1992.

[2] Abū ʿUbayd al-Qāsim b. al-Sallām, *Kitāb al-Amwāl*, p. 543 §1997.

state became jobless, old, or disabled then they would be legally entitled to social benefit and income support."[1]

This model of conduct was also adopted by the Caliphs of the Prophet ﷺ. For instance, ʿUmar b. al-Khaṭṭāb ؓ saw an old Jewish citizen of Medina begging and he asked him: "Why are you begging?" The Jew replied: "I have to pay the tax that's why I am begging and I am jobless." ʿUmar ؓ helped him financially. He then sent him to the secretary of finance and said: "From today all Jews, Christians and non-Muslims who are jobless or who are old and unable to earn are exempted from the national taxes for their security and they are entitled to income support and social benefit."[2]

1.9.7 Jews and Christians Enjoyed a Multicultural Coexistence in Muslim Lands

Throughout Islamic history both Jews and Christians enjoyed hostile-free existence in Muslim lands. In cases where injustices have been committed against the non-Muslims by the Muslims, orders have been passed against the latter to correct their wrongs. al-Balādharī says in *Futūḥ al-Buldān* (p. 150), that during ʿUmar b. ʿAbd al-ʿAzīz's caliphate a part of a church was demolished and included into a mosque. The case was referred to the Caliph who ordered that the part of the mosque should be demolished and the land returned to the Christians so that they could re-build their church.

These are a handful of examples to illustrate the position accorded to non-Muslims in an Islamic state. Islam teaches respect for other religions and it holds itself responsible for the protection of churches and other places of worship. In the Islamic state Christians were permitted to sing Christmas songs

[1] Abū Yūsuf, *Kitāb al-Kharāj*, pp. 122, 125.

[2] Ibn Qudāma, *al-Mughnī*, vol. 8, pp. 507–511; Abū Yūsuf, *Kitāb al-Kharāj*, p. 125.

during Christmas except for at the time of the five obligatory prayers. Islamic rule commanded that their religion, culture and practice should never be interfered with and that they should enjoy complete religious freedom.

Moreover there were written instructions from the Holy Prophet ﷺ and the Caliphs that non-Muslims would never be forced to perform state defence duties, but their protection was the responsibility of the state.[1] Military commanders were given a commandment by Abū Bakr which has been reported by al-Bayhaqī, that during wartime the captured lands of non-Muslims should come to no harm. The trees should not be cut, their cattle should not be killed and their places of worship should not be demolished. If religious leaders were confined in the act of worship in their churches they should not be disturbed as they are not combatants. No harm should be caused to even the general population in their homes.[2]

In light of the primary evidences and its substantiations presented above it is manifest that those 'Muslims' who adhere to ideologies of violence and indiscriminate killings, and those who condone suicide bombings, all in the name of Islam, are most certainly not adherents of the Prophetic paradigm.

1.10 The Treaty of udaybiyya: A Shining Symbol of the Prophetic Preference for Peace over Conflict

An interesting case study of the Prophet's conduct in times of tension and turbulence, is the occasion of the *Treaty of Ḥudaybiyya*. In the year 628, the Prophet Muhammad ﷺ set out to perform the pilgrimage, with about 1400 unarmed companions, dressed in two pieces of unsown cloth, known

[1] al-Kāsānī, *al-Badāʾiʿ wa al-Ṣanāʾiʿ*, vol. 7, pp. 112, 113; al-Shurbīnī, *Mughnī al-Muḥtāj*, vol. 4, p. 243.

[2] Related by al-Bayhaqī in *al-Sunan al-Kubrā*, vol. 9, p. 85 §17904.

as the *iḥrām*. Upon hearing of the Prophet's intentions, the Meccan leaders and neighbouring tribes took up arms and were determined to deter the Muslims from entering the Holy vicinity. The Meccan armies, together with their allies, marched out of Mecca and awaited the Prophet's arrival. When the Muslims arrived at Ḥudaybiyya, a place several miles from Mecca, the Prophet ﷺ ordered the Muslims to camp, and then selected ʿUthmān b. ʿAffān ؓ as his emissary, to go and negotiate with the Meccan leaders, which ultimately proved unsuccessful. Finally, the Meccans sent a delegation headed by Suhayl b. ʿAmr, and the negotiations resulted in the Treaty of Ḥudaybiyya.

Under the terms of the treaty, the Prophet Muhammad ﷺ would be allowed to make the pilgrimage the following year and was thus denied entry into Mecca. The holy vicinity would be emptied for three days for the Muslim pilgrims. The treaty also stipulated a truce for ten years. Any tribe or person would be free to join either party or make an alliance with it; the slaves amongst the Meccans, who had left paganism and accepted Islam were to be returned to the Meccans by the Muslims.

This last condition was not reciprocal and was objected to in the Muslim camp. Senior Companions such as ʿUmar b. al-Khaṭṭāb ؓ were shocked that the Prophet ﷺ could accept such a biased stipulation. The Prophet Muhammad ﷺ responded to all objections with wisdom and told his followers that they would understand the reasons behind his decisions. As the treaty was signed, Abū Jandal, the son of Suhayl, the head of the Meccan delegation, came, trailing his chains, in order to join the Muslims. God's Messenger ﷺ had to return him to his father in tears, in order to abide by the conditions of the treaty. This again upset the Prophet's ﷺ followers and again he taught them to be patient and await success from God.

Prophet Muhammad ﷺ asked ʿAlī ؓ to write down the

treaty and Suhayl b. ʿAmr a representative of the Meccans witnessed it. Upon noticing that the treaty began in the Name of God, Suhayl objected and asserted that it be removed. The Prophet Muhammad ﷺ instructed ʿAlī to remove it. Suhayl again objected when ʿAlī ؓ wrote the name of the Prophet Muhammad with the appellation 'the Messenger of God'. The Prophet ﷺ instructed 'Ali to remove it, but he could not bring himself to do so. The Prophet ﷺ then took it upon himself to comply with the demand of the Meccans. By doing thus, neither was his prophecy negated nor did it lower his status in the eyes of those around him. In fact, his conduct amplified his nobility further and as with all his noble acts, this was also a harbinger of peace.

Another condition of the treaty, which was not favourable to the Muslims, was to return to Medina without having performed the pilgrimage. The Prophet ﷺ instructed his followers to remove their *iḥrām* and sacrifice their animals but none of the followers complied. They were in a state of shock and distressed at having reached their destination only to turn away without having fulfilled their purpose. Thrice Prophet Muhammad ﷺ instructed them and all three times they refused to obey. Upon the advice of his wife Umm Salama ؓ the Prophet ﷺ removed his *iḥrām* and slaughtered his camel. Upon seeing this, the Companions removed their *iḥrām* and sacrificed an animal.[1]

These strategic actions undertaken by Prophet Muhammad ﷺ only reinforced the belief his followers had in his message and enhanced the security of his people. Complying with the Meccans, to engender peace and security, was his main objective and by acquiescing to their demands this lofty objective was achieved.

---

[1] Related by al-Bukhārī in *al-Saḥīḥ*, vol. 2, pp. 974–979 §2580.

1.11 The West and Muslim Minorities

1.11.1 Understanding and Tackling Extremism and Terrorism

If the West truly wishes to eliminate terrorism they must begin by identifying their enemies. These terrorists are no more than a handful of misguided people whose religious life is based either on misinterpretation or ignorance of the religious teachings. It is also important that they do not confine extremism to Islam, or any other religion for that matter, for it is found amongst followers of all religious traditions. Extremism has no religion and it most certainly has no place in Islam. Rather, terrorism is an attitude and a social behaviour, which arises from frustration and nihilism.

The incessant attempts to connect Islam and terrorism, as though they are absolutely inseparable, has led to the infusion of antagonism in the hearts and minds of young Muslims; hence the widespread expressions of hatred and animosity. The West must also discontinue its support for Muslim countries with extremist attitudes. I personally know of many countries that not only financially support extremists and their projects but also provide them with political protection. The causes of terrorism are multifarious and it is the underlying causes that must be tackled; be they political, psychological or sociological.

1.11.2 Muslims: Integration, Isolation, or Annihilation

The Medinan society, established by the Prophet Muhammad ﷺ himself, was built on the principle of integration and was as such a categorical rejection of the models of isolation and annihilation, the former of which would have left his community cut off from the rest of the world and the latter, devoid of a definite identity, unique to them.

Muslims living in Britain, America and Europe have a choice. They either follow the path the Prophet Muhammad ﷺ took and integrate into the British society by abiding by the law of the land, participating in the political process, and at the same time fulfil their obligations as Muslims. In contradistinction, they may go against the Prophet's teachings and instead, live in ghettoised areas, hostile to other communities and unwilling to participate in any form of communal structure. Views and propagations that suggest such ideologies are to be shunned and abandoned in their entirety.

1.11.3 CLOSING: THE PROPHET'S FINAL SERMON—A FORERUNNER TO THE UNIVERSAL DECLARATION OF HUMAN RIGHTS

In his Farewell Sermon, the Prophet Muhammad ﷺ addressed a gathering of more than a hundred thousand people, summarising his teachings for them, as well as reminding them of his life-long struggle in upholding the highest moral principles that humankind ever witnessed. In this historic sermon, he spoke of racial equality, tolerance and peace. In fact the basis for a declaration of human rights was established through this sermon alone. Superiority of one human being over any other was quashed, except by individual excellence and conscientiousness. Thus excellence of moral character was to be the only criterion of individual superiority in the eyes of God. The rights of each and every human being pertaining to their person, property and honour were declared sacrosanct.

At the domestic front, his sermon banished oppression and centuries of subjugation of women by declaring them as equals to men.

Before his arrival, Arabia was fraught with deceit and corruption in trade and commerce, so he eliminated economic exploitation by enforcing just trade, as well as the right to ownership and inheritance. He declared fulfilling the rights of the state an obligation upon all Muslims, thus ensuring that they live as peaceful citizens wherever they may be. His message was not only for the thousands standing before him but for Muslims of all places and times. It was a universal message, whose teachings resonate in the corners of the earth, such that the Universal Declaration of Human Rights is based on the same concepts.

This is a brief exposition of the magnanimous conduct of the Prophet of Islam. The reality is that no amount of words can truly capture the grandeur of that Man whose noble teachings gave rise to an empire of peace and mercy. The Qurʾān and the Prophetic Sunna are his legacy and will last forever, thus ensuring that every age will see for itself the miracles of his conduct.

PART TWO

RENOUNCING TERROR, REGAINING PEACE, AND THE FUTURE OF ISLAM

2.1 Author's Preface

This lecture will put the three parts of the title together into a single coherent narrative with the aim of imbuing greater clarity and lucidity than if they were addressed separately. There is no doubt that we are living in a crucial and critical time, with the Muslim community as a whole, and the younger generation in particular, facing a terrible situation in connection to their Islamic faith, particularly in the West. A monstrous image of the faith has been painted by the media, creating misunderstanding and confusion amongst both Muslims and non-Muslims. Likewise, those who are engaged in the propagation of Islam and its defence, act in a way that does not serve the Islamic objectives but rather plays into the hands of their antagonists. Instead of imitating this approach, in order to understand this case in the light of the basic teachings and prescriptions of Islam it would be better to refer the whole case to the Qur'ān, Sunna and the *sīra* of the Holy Prophet Muhammad ﷺ. Thus this discourse will be clarifying the true essence of Islam commencing with its lexical meaning, thereafter going onto its true nature and basic teachings with the intention of determining where this noble religion stands in connection to peace and terrorism.

2.2 Lexical and Technical Meanings of Islam, *Īmān*, and *Iḥsān*

There are three basic postulations that underpin Islamic thought: Islam, *īmān*, and *iḥsān*. Islam is the practical dimension of the religion which deals with the outward; *īmān* is its theological dimension which deals with thoughts and beliefs; and *iḥsān* is the spiritual dimension, concerned with achieving internal excellence and perfection. As for the lexical implications of these words it is interesting to note that the word Islam is derived from the root word *silm*, which denotes peace, discipline and obedience,[1] whilst the word *īmān* is derived from the root word *aman* and *amn* which signifies peace, safety and security.[2] *Iḥsān* is derived from *ḥusn* which means excellence and beauty.[3] Before we proceed in elaborating this concept it is necessary to repel a misgiving when discussing the significance of peace in the Islamic teachings and when rejecting terrorism. There are primarily two kinds of reactions to this discussion: the first is of the sceptics who do not understand the real teachings of the religion, holding the misguided viewpoint that any discussion on the concept of peace in Islam as nothing but a mere strategy aiming to give a peaceful face to the tradition; the second is of a number of Muslims themselves who, when hearing talk of peace, assume that Muslims have become apologetic in the face of Western aggression and that there is no need to become defensive. To clarify, this essay is neither a defence strategy nor is it apologetic: it is an attempt to relay the real message of Islam.

To begin with Islam, Almighty Allah and the Prophet Muhammad ﷺ have declared that the best of Islam is to propagate and practice peace, having stated:

«تُطْعِمُ الطَّعَامَ وَتَقْرَأُ السَّلَامَ عَلَى مَنْ عَرَفْتَ وَمَنْ لَمْ تَعْرِفْ».

(The best action in Islam is that) you serve the food, and recite the salutation of peace to someone whether

---

1 Ibn Manẓūr, *Lisān al-ʿArab*, vol. 12, p. 289.

2 Ibn Manẓūr, *Lisān al-ʿArab*, vol. 13, p. 21.

3 Abū Manṣūr al-Azharī, *Tahdhīb al-Lugha*, vol. 4, p. 182; Ibn Manẓūr, *Lisān al-ʿArab*, vol. 13, p. 114.

you know him or do not know![1]

In emulation of this noble precinct set by the Prophet Muhammad ﷺ, Muslims greet with the formula of peace: *al-sālam-u ʿalaykum* meaning 'peace be unto you', and conclude prayers by uttering the words of peace when turning one's head to the right and the left: *al-sālam-u ʿalaykum wa raḥmatʾul-llāh* which translates to 'peace be upon you and mercy of Allah.' This is a proclamation of peace to those sat on either side. Similarly, when the believers enter the gates of Paradise they will be greeted with the words of peace as recorded in the Qurʾān. Almighty Allah and the angels will receive them saying,

﴿تَحِيَّتُهُمْ يَوْمَ يَلْقَوْنَهُۥ سَلَٰمٌ﴾

﴾On the Day when they (the believers) will meet Ḥim, their gift (of the meeting — greeting) will be: 'Peace!'﴿[2]

The epithet of Paradise, as given by Almighty Allah, is *Dār al-Salām*, or 'the abode of peace'. Among the many names and attributes of God, one of the most significant is the name *al-Salām*, the source of peace. After each prayer in conformity to the noble practice of the Prophet Muhammad ﷺ, the Muslims plead unto God, invoking Him with the following supplication:

«اللَّهُمَّ أَنْتَ السَّلَامُ وَمِنْكَ السَّلَامُ، تَبَارَكْتَ يا ذَا الْجَلَالِ وَالْإِكْرَامِ».

O Allah: You are Peace, and peace comes from You,

---

[1] Related by al-Bukhārī in *al-Ṣaḥīḥ*, vol. 1, pp. 13, 19 §12, 28; and Muslim in *al-Ṣaḥīḥ*, vol. 1, p. 65 §39.

[2] Qurʾān 33:44.

> blessed are You, Possessor of Glory and Honour.[1]

In another narration related by Makḥūl and transmitted by al-Bayhaqī, it is stated when the Holy Prophet ﷺ entered Mecca and saw the House of Allah, he raised his hands, glorified the greatness and majesty of Almighty Allah and prayed with these words:

«اللَّهُمَّ أَنْتَ السَّلَامُ وَمِنْكَ السَّلَامُ، فَحَيِّنَا رَبَّنَا بِالسَّلَامِ».

> O Allah: You are Peace, and peace comes from You.
> O our Lord! Give us a life of peace.[2]

The three words Islam, *īmān*, and *iḥsān* originate from the famous *Tradition of Gabriel*, in which he came to the Prophet ﷺ in the guise of a Bedouin to teach the Companions ﷺ their religion. The tradition related by ʿUmar b. al-Khaṭṭāb ﷺ is as follows:

بَيْنَمَا نَحْنُ عِنْدَ رَسُوْلِ اللهِ ﷺ ذَاتَ يَوْمٍ إِذْ طَلَعَ عَلَيْنَا رَجُلٌ شَدِيْدُ بَيَاضِ الثِّيَابِ، شَدِيْدُ سَوَادِ الشَّعْرِ. لَا يُرَى عَلَيْهِ أَثَرُ السَّفَرِ، وَلَا يَعْرِفُهُ مِنَّا أَحَدٌ، حَتَّى جَلَسَ إِلَى النَّبِيِّ ﷺ، فَأَسْنَدَ رُكْبَتَيْهِ إِلَى رُكْبَتَيْهِ، وَوَضَعَ كَفَّيْهِ عَلَى فَخِذَيْهِ، وَقَالَ: يَا مُحَمَّدُ! أَخْبِرْنِي عَنِ الإِسْلَامِ. فَقَالَ رَسُوْلُ اللهِ ﷺ: «الإِسْلَامُ أَنْ تَشْهَدَ أَنْ لَا إِلَهَ إِلَّا اللهُ، وَأَنَّ مُحَمَّدًا رَسُوْلُ اللهِ، وَتُقِيمَ الصَّلَاةَ، وَتُؤْتِيَ الزَّكَاةَ، وَتَصُوْمَ رَمَضَانَ، وَتَحُجَّ الْبَيْتَ إِنِ اسْتَطَعْتَ إِلَيْهِ سَبِيْلًا».

---

[1] Related by Muslim in *al-Ṣaḥīḥ*, vol. 1, p. 414 §591, 592; Abū Dāwūd in *al-Sunan*, vol. 1, p. 474 §1512; al-Tirmidhī in *al-Sunan*, vol. 2, p. 95, §298; al-Nasāʾī in *al-Sunan*, vol. 3, pp. 68, 69 §1337, 1338; Ibn Mājah in *al-Sunan*, vol. 1, pp. 298, 300 §924, 928.

[2] Related by al-Bayhaqī in *al-Sunan al-Kubrā*, vol. 5, p. 73 §8995.

قَالَ: صَدَقْتَ. قَالَ: فَعَجِبْنَا لَهُ يَسْأَلُهُ وَيُصَدِّقُهُ! قَالَ: فَأَخْبِرْنِي
عَنِ الإِيْمَانِ. قَالَ: «أَنْ تُؤْمِنَ بِاللهِ، وَمَلاَئِكَتِهِ، وَكُتُبِهِ، وَرُسُلِهِ،
وَالْيَوْمِ الآخِرِ، وَتُؤْمِنَ بِالْقَدَرِ خَيْرِهِ وَشَرِّهِ». قَالَ: صَدَقْتَ.
قَالَ: فَأَخْبِرْنِي عَنِ الإِحْسَانِ. قَالَ: «أَنْ تَعْبُدَ اللهَ كَأَنَّكَ تَرَاهُ،
فَإِنْ لَمْ تَكُنْ تَرَاهُ فَإِنَّهُ يَرَاكَ». ... ثُمَّ انْطَلَقَ، فَلَبِثْتُ مَلِيّاً، ثُمَّ قَالَ:
يَا عُمَرُ! «أَتَدْرِي مَنِ السَّائِلُ»؟ قُلتُ: اللهُ وَرَسُوْلُهُ أَعْلَمُ. قَالَ:
«فَإِنَّهُ جِبْرِيْلُ، أَتَاكُمْ يُعَلِّمُكُمْ دِيْنَكُمْ».

As we sat one day with the Messenger of Allah ﷺ, a man in pure white clothing and jet black hair came to us, without a trace of travelling upon him, though none of us knew him. He sat down before the Prophet ﷺ bracing his knees against his, resting his hands on his legs, and said: " O Muhammad, tell me about Islam." The Messenger of Allah ﷺ said: "Islam is to testify that there is no God but Allah and that Muhammad is the Messenger of Allah, and to perform the prayer, give Zakat, fast in Ramaḍān, and perform the pilgrimage to the House if you can find a way." He said: "You have spoken the truth," and we were surprised that he should ask and then confirm the answer. Then he said: "Tell me about true faith (*īmān*)" and the Prophet ﷺ answered: "It is to believe in Allah, His angels, His inspired Books, His messengers, the Last Day, and in destiny, it's good and evil." "You have spoken the truth," he said, "Now tell me about the perfection of faith (*iḥsān*)," and the Prophet ﷺ answered: "It is to worship Allah as if you see Him, and if you see Him not, He nevertheless sees you." ... Then the visitor left. I

> waited a long while, and the Prophet ﷺ said to me, "Do you know, ʿUmar, who was the questioner?" and I replied, "Allah and His Messenger know best." He said, "It was Gabriel, who came to you to teach you your religion." [1]

These three terms (which are three grades of the religion of Islam as well) were also spoken by God in the Qurʾān, and it is interesting to note that Almighty Allah has chosen specific words to prescribe and illustrate the concept of Islam, *īmān* and *iḥsān*.

Concerning *Islam*, the first grade of Islam, God says in the Qurʾān:

﴿ٱلْيَوْمَ أَكْمَلْتُ لَكُمْ دِينَكُمْ وَأَتْمَمْتُ عَلَيْكُمْ نِعْمَتِي
وَرَضِيتُ لَكُمُ ٱلْإِسْلَٰمَ دِينًا﴾

﴾Today I have perfected for you your religion and I have completed the bestowal of My mercy upon you, and I am pleased to choose Islam as your religion.﴿[2]

Here the word *raḍītu* (derived from *riḍā*; pleasure) is linked with the word Islam. Likewise concerning the second grade of Islam, *īmān*, the Qurʾān states:

﴿قَالَتِ ٱلْأَعْرَابُ ءَامَنَّا ۖ قُل لَّمْ تُؤْمِنُوا۟ وَلَٰكِن قُولُوٓا۟ أَسْلَمْنَا

---

[1] Related by al-Bukhārī in *al-Ṣaḥīḥ*, vol. 1, p. 27 §50; vol. 4, p. 1793 §4499; Muslim in *al-Ṣaḥīḥ*, vol. 1, p. 36 §8, 9; al-Tirmidhī in *al-Sunan*, vol. 5, p. 6 §2610, Abū Dāwūd in *al-Sunan*, vol. 4, p. 359 §4697; al-Nasāʾī in *al-Sunan*, vol. 8, p. 97 §4990; Ibn Mājah in *al-Sunan*, vol. 1, p. 24 §63; Aḥmad b. Ḥanbal in *al-Musnad*, vol. 1, p. 51 §367; Ibn Khuzayma in *al-Ṣaḥīḥ*, vol. 4, p. 127 §2504; and Ibn Ḥibbān in *al-Ṣaḥīḥ*, vol. 1, p. 389 §168.

[2] Qurʾān 5:3.

وَلَمَّا يَدۡخُلِ ٱلۡإِيمَٰنُ فِي قُلُوبِكُمۡۖ﴾

﴿The Bedouins say: 'We have believed.' Say: 'You have not believed. Yes, rather say: We have accepted Islam. And the belief has not yet gone into your hearts.'﴾ [1]

At another place, the Qur'ān states about the second grade of Islam in these words:

﴿وَلَٰكِنَّ ٱللَّهَ حَبَّبَ إِلَيۡكُمُ ٱلۡإِيمَٰنَ وَزَيَّنَهُۥ فِي قُلُوبِكُمۡ﴾

﴿But Allah has blessed you with the love of faith and has embellished it in your hearts.﴾ [2]

In this verse, Almighty Allah has chosen two words to explain *īmān*; one is *maḥabba* (love) and the other is *zīna* (beauty).

Finally, *iḥsān*, which is the third and excellent grade of the religion of Islam, is imbued with the concept of eliminating mischief and corruption from the world. Almighty Allah states:

﴿وَأَحۡسِن كَمَآ أَحۡسَنَ ٱللَّهُ إِلَيۡكَۖ وَلَا تَبۡغِ ٱلۡفَسَادَ فِي ٱلۡأَرۡضِۖ﴾

﴿And do (such) good (to the people) as Allah has done good to you. But do not look for (ways to spread) evil and terror in the land (through oppression, accumulation of wealth and exploitation).﴾ [3]

In this verse *iḥsān* has been connected with negation of *fasād*, i.e. this verse instructs the believer to adopt the practice of *iḥsān* and thus eliminate corruption from the world. The

1 Qur'ān 49:14.

2 Qur'ān 49:7.

3 Qur'ān 28:77.

choice of words used to illustrate the concepts of *Islam, īmān and iḥsān* therefore pose a significant relevance.

Also noteworthy are the definitions of a Muslim and a *muʾmin*, meaning a true believer, as explained by the Prophet Muhammad ﷺ.

According to ʿAbd Allāh b. ʿAmr b. al-ʿĀṣ ؓ, Allah's Messenger ﷺ said:

«اَلْمُسْلِمُ مَنْ سَلِمَ الْـمُسْلِمُوْنَ مِنْ لِسَانِهِ وَيَدِهِ».

> A Muslim is the one who provides peace to other Muslims through his words and deeds. [1]

A *muʾmin* was described as:

«اَلْمُؤْمِنُ مَنْ أَمِنَهُ النَّاسُ عَلَى دِمَائِهِمْ وَأَمْوَالِهِمْ».

> The *muʾmin* is someone whom people trust with regard to their blood and their properties. [2]

Thus, a true believer is the one who provides peace and security for not only Muslims but non-Muslims alike.

In another tradition transmitted by Shaddād b. Aws ؓ, the Prophet ﷺ said of *iḥsān*:

«إِنَّ اللهَ كَتَبَ الإِحْسَانَ عَلَى كُلِّ شَيءٍ، فَإِذَا قَتَلْتُمْ فَأَحْسِنُوا الْقِتْلَةَ، وَإِذَا ذَبَحْتُمْ فَأَحْسِنُوا الذَّبحَ، وَلْيُحِدَّ أَحَدُكُمْ شَفْرَتَهُ، فَلْيُـرِحْ ذَبِيْحَتَهُ».

---

[1] Related by al-Bukhārī in *al-Ṣaḥīḥ*, vol. 1, p. 13 §10; Muslim in *al-Ṣaḥīḥ*, vol. 1, p. 65 §41; al-Tirmidhī in *al-Sunan*, vol. 5, p. 17 §2627; Aḥmad b. Ḥanbal in *al-Musnad*, vol. 3, p. 440 §15673; and Ibn Ḥibbān in *al-Ṣaḥīḥ*, vol. 1, p. 406 §180.

[2] Related by al-Nasāʾī in *al-Sunan*, vol. 8, p. 104 §4995; and Aḥmad b. Ḥanbal in *al-Musnad*, vol. 2, p. 379 §8918.

> Allah has prescribed spiritual excellence in the treatment of everything, so if you kill (any combatant during war), you must perform the killing with moral excellence (causing the least torture), and if you sacrifice an animal, you must perform the slaughter most caringly, and let one of you sharpen his blade, in order to set his sacrificial animal at rest (causing it least discomfort)![1]

In a state of war disposition for benevolence is commanded and at the same time infliction of terror is sternly prohibited. In the same cruelty to animals is also forbidden even during slaughter.

Furthermore, the Prophet ﷺ said:

«اَلْخَلْقُ كُلُّهُمْ عِيَالُ اللهِ، فَأَحَبُّ الْخَلْقِ إِلَى اللهِ أَنْفَعُهُمْ لِعِيَالِهِ».

> The whole of creation is the dependent (family) of Allah. So the dearest one to Him, from amongst them, is the one most beneficial to His family.[2]

2.3 THE CONCEPT OF BALANCE IN ISLAM

The aforementioned traditions are a brief exposition of the concepts and implications of Islam, *īmān*, and *iḥsān*. What follows now is a brief discourse on the concepts of balance,

---

[1] Related by Muslim in *al-Ṣaḥīḥ*, vol. 3, p. 1548 §1955; al-Tirmidhī in *al-Sunan*, vol. 4, p. 23 §1409; Abū Dāwūd in *al-Sunan*, vol. 3, p. 58 §2817; al-Nasāʾī in *al-Sunan*, vol. 7, p. 227 §4405; and Ibn Mājah in *al-Sunan*, vol. 2, p. 1058 §3170.

[2] Related by al-Ṭabarānī in *al-Muʿjam al-Kabīr*, vol. 10, p. 86 §10033, and *al-Muʿjam al-Awsaṭ*, vol. 5, p. 356 §5541; Abū Yaʿlā in *al-Musnad*, vol. 6, pp. 65, 106, 194 §3315, 3370, 3478; al-Shāshī in *al-Musnad*, vol. 1, p. 419 §435; and al-Qaḍāʿī in *Musnad al-Shihāb*, vol. 2, p. 255 §1306.

tolerance and moderation in light of the Qur᾿ān and Prophetic tradition.

The Holy Qur᾿ān explains that,

﴿وَلَقَدْ خَلَقْنَا ٱلْإِنسَـٰنَ مِن سُلَـٰلَةٍ مِّن طِينٍ ۝١٢ ثُمَّ جَعَلْنَـٰهُ
نُطْفَةً فِى قَرَارٍ مَّكِينٍ ۝١٣ ثُمَّ خَلَقْنَا ٱلنُّطْفَةَ عَلَقَةً فَخَلَقْنَا ٱلْعَلَقَةَ
مُضْغَةً فَخَلَقْنَا ٱلْمُضْغَةَ عِظَـٰمًا فَكَسَوْنَا ٱلْعِظَـٰمَ لَحْمًا ثُمَّ
أَنشَأْنَـٰهُ خَلْقًا ءَاخَرَ ۚ فَتَبَارَكَ ٱللَّهُ أَحْسَنُ ٱلْخَـٰلِقِينَ﴾

﴿*And indeed We originated (the genesis of) man from the extract of (chemical ingredients of) clay. Then We placed him as a sperm drop (zygote) in a secure place (mother's womb). Then We made that zygote a hanging mass (clinging to the uterus like a leech). Then We developed that hanging mass into a lump, looking chewed with teeth. Out of this chewed lump We built a structure of bones which We clothed with flesh (and muscles). Then (changing him) into another form We developed him (gradually) into a new creation. Then Allah brought (him up into a strong body), Allah — the Best of creators.*﴾[1]

﴿أَيَحْسَبُ ٱلْإِنسَـٰنُ أَن يُتْرَكَ سُدًى ۝٣٦ أَلَمْ يَكُ نُطْفَةً مِّن مَّنِىٍّ
يُمْنَىٰ ۝٣٧ ثُمَّ كَانَ عَلَقَةً فَخَلَقَ فَسَوَّىٰ﴾

﴿*Does man think that he will be left for nothing (without any reckoning)? Was he not (in his beginning) a sperm drop ejaculated (into the woman's womb)? Then it developed into a hanging*

---

[1] Qur᾿ān 23:12–14.

mass (clinging to the womb like a nest). Then He created (in it the preliminary form of all the limbs of the body). Then He set (them) right.﴿[1]

The human body is in a state of equilibrium; the organs and both the mental and spiritual faculties are perfectly balanced. The question is why has God created this balance? The answer is because this balance allows man to achieve a state of peace, tolerance and security, and through it the faculties of human personality are able to work together in an atmosphere of mutual interaction and co-operation which is conducive to human life.

How can this balance be achieved? God has created in man various facets to his personality; he is a multidimensional being. He has a biological dimension, whilst at the same time he is bound and responsible for the social aspects of his life; he has a spiritual dimension ingrained into his personality whilst at the same time he must deal with the philosophical and intellectual realities of his being. Any imbalance in any of these faculties is regarded as un-Islamic; Islam recommends its followers to fulfil the due requirements of each aspect of human personality so that a balance is achieved; when these requirements are met, peace, tranquillity and tolerance are the final outcome.

A believer must fulfil the rights of his Creator, the rights of the Prophet ﷺ, the rights of his own person and the rights of society. Progress in one's spiritual life should not occur at the neglect of one's secular obligations, such a monastic approach to life is prohibited in Islam. Similarly, development in one's secular life must not occur at the detriment of one's spiritual and religious needs. Any form of behaviour which has the potential to create an imbalance in one's personality or generate extremist tendencies is prohibited in Islam. We should

[1] Qur'ān 75:36–38.

aim to create a balance within our lives so that when we are confronted by secularists the innate beauty of a believer's secular life shines forth and at the same time the spiritualist should be affected by the believer's spiritual beauty. An example of this is present in the life of the Prophet Muhammad ﷺ who interacted with both the young and old and participated in social activities with full vigour.

Tradition notes that the Prophet Muhammad ﷺ was actively involved in the popular physical sports of the time, including swimming,[1] horse riding[2] and wrestling,[3] yet at the same time he was a man of great spirituality and in proximity to God. This is the lifestyle that a Muslim must adopt in order to live in harmony with oneself and others. Disapproval of a monastic existence is evident in one tradition when the Prophet ﷺ enquired a woman about her marriage and relationship to her husband. She responded that he was a very pious individual who would stand the whole night in prayer, and spend the whole day in state of fasting. Upon hearing this, the Prophet ﷺ rebuked the husband for his conduct,[4] informing him that his wife had rights over him as well as God[5] and that he must

---

[1] Related by Abū Nuʿaym in *Ḥilya al-Awliyā'*, vol. 1, p. 184; and al-Hindī in *Kanz al-ʿUmmāl*, vol. 16, 184 §45345.

[2] Related by al-Bukhārī in *al-Ṣaḥīḥ*, vol. 2, p. 835 §2242; and vol. 3, pp. 1050, 1332 §2705, 3446; Muslim in *al-Ṣaḥīḥ*, vol. 2, pp. 680, 681 §987; and al-Nasā'ī in *al-Sunan*, vol. 6, p. 216 §3563.

[3] Related by Ibn Kathīr in *al-Bidāya wa al-Nihāya*, vol. 3, pp. 103, 104; al-Qasṭallānī in *al-Mawāhib al-Laduniyya*, vol. 2, p. 365; and al-Zurqānī in *Sharḥ al-Mawāhib al-Laduniyya*, vol. 4, p. 292.

[4] Related by Aḥmad b. Ḥanbal in *al-Musnad*, vol. 6, p. 226 §25935; Ibn Ḥibbān in *al-Ṣaḥīḥ*, vol. 1, p. 185 §9; ʿAbd al-Razzāq in *al-Muṣannaf*, vol. 6, pp. 167, 168 §10375, and vol. 7, p. 150 §12591; and al-Ṭabarānī in *al-Muʿjam al-Kabir*, vol. 9, p. 38 §8319.

[5] Related by al-Bukhārī in *al-Ṣaḥīḥ*, vol. 2, pp. 696, 697 §1873, 1874; Muslim in *al-Ṣaḥīḥ*, vol. 2, p. 813 §1159; and Aḥmad b. Ḥanbal in *al-Musnad*, vol. 2, p. 198.

fulfil the rights of both in order to live a balanced life.

The same beauty and balance described regarding the human personality is also apparent in the celestial order of the universe. Almighty Allah has created the whole of this universe on the same principle of balance:

﴿ثُمَّ ٱسْتَوَىٰٓ إِلَى ٱلسَّمَآءِ وَهِىَ دُخَانٌ فَقَالَ لَهَا وَلِلْأَرْضِ ٱئْتِيَا
طَوْعًا أَوْ كَرْهًا قَالَتَآ أَتَيْنَا طَآئِعِينَ﴾

﴾Then He turned towards the heavenly universe—that was (all) smoke. So He said to it (the heavenly spheres) and the earth: "Get in (compliance with Our system) either under the influence of mutual attraction and coordination or under aversion and revulsion." Both said: "We submit with pleasure.'﴿[1]

There is no conflict between the heavens and the earth; the celestial order that has been placed by Almighty Allah is in a state of balance thereby creating peace. So in the same way that Allah has provided balance within our human personality and the celestial system around us, it is expected from us, as stewards and trustees of the divine will, to act accordingly with the world around us.

These examples simply convey one message that Islam rejects any kind of extremist tendency in life; regardless of whether extremism is in a positive or negative manner. This then leads to the wondering of how Islam condones terrorism. Acts of terrorism are the result of radicalisation and radicalism is the result of extremism, so if Islam does not allow extremism in one's life then how can it possibly allow terrorism? The causes of terrorism must be investigated; bracketing the Muslim community or Islam with terrorism must be avoided. Terrorism

---

[1] Qur'ān 41:11.

has no link to any religion; it is a social, psychological and economic phenomenon which transcends all barriers of race, religion and culture. Extremists and fanatics have not only existed within Muslims cultures, they have also existed in Western cultures; for this reason every society must search for and uproot all causes and motives which lead to acts of terror.

To further scrutinise Islam's stance on violence and terrorism one need only examine the character and personality of the Prophet Muhammad ﷺ. When he migrated to Medina a written document was prepared known as the Constitution of Medina; this was one of the first constitutions ever written. The Constitution of Medina formed the basis of a just and peaceful society under the leadership of the Prophet Muhammad ﷺ and it was pivotal in the eradication of terrorist and extremist activities that had plagued the Arabian Peninsula for centuries.

At the time there were two major tribes residing in Medina: the Aws and Khazraj; alongside these two tribes were another eight who were allied to one of them, and thirty-three other groups that existed. In total no less than forty-three different factions existed in Medina when the Prophet ﷺ migrated there. Through the Constitution of Medina, the Prophet ﷺ was able to establish a multiethnic and a multicultural society which he administered as the head of state. A full-fledged charter was provided, which brought about cooperation in aspects of defence, finance, society and politics. Under his leadership, an atmosphere of mutual cooperation was achieved which respected local customary laws; it was an atmosphere which recognised rights for the freedom of religion and culture, with minorities being granted rights to practice their own religion.

One noteworthy example is when a large delegation of Christians from Najrān visited the Prophet ﷺ in Medina, he received them with great hospitality and allowed them to reside at his Mosque. When they desired to worship, the Prophet ﷺ

offered them the use of his Mosque.[1] The delegation did not come to Medina to have a peaceful dialogue with the Prophet ﷺ for purposes of mutual understanding. Rather they came with the intention of debating with him to rebut his teachings. This is just one example of who the West must turn to in order to achieve greater understanding of Islamic teachings.

The sermon delivered by the Prophet ﷺ during the farewell pilgrimage, is another example of Islam's position on toleration and peace. This sermon was the beginning of a new world order which marked an age grounded in mutual cooperation and peace. The Prophet ﷺ spoke:

«أَلَا كُلُّ شَيْءٍ مِنْ أَمْرِ الْجَاهِلِيَّةِ تَحْتَ قَدَمَيَّ مَوْضُوعٌ».

> Be aware! All matters pertaining to the age of jāhiliyya (an age of exploitation and oppression) had been trampled under my feet.[2]

This declaration marked the beginning of a new system which was to be based on justice and human dignity; it was a system that was designated to bring about equality amongst mankind. The Prophet ﷺ continued with,

«إِنَّ دِمَاءَكُمْ وَأَمْوَالَكُمْ حَرَامٌ عَلَيْكُمْ كَحُرْمَةِ يَوْمِكُمْ هَذَا، فِي شَهْرِكُمْ هَذَا، فِي بَلَدِكُمْ هَذَا».

> (O mankind!) Indeed your lives and properties have been sanctified like the sanctity of this holy day, and

---

[1] Related by Ibn Saʿd in *al-Ṭabaqāt al-Kubrā*, vol. 1, p. 357; and Ibn al-Qayyim in *Zād al-Maʿād*, vol. 3, p. 629.

[2] Related by Muslim in *al-Ṣaḥīḥ*, vol. 2, p. 889 §1218; Abū Dāwūd in *al-Sunan*, vol. 2, p. 185 §1905; Ibn Ḥibbān in *al-Ṣaḥīḥ*, vol. 9, .p. 257 §3944; al-Nasāʾī in *al-Sunan*, vo. 2, p. 421 §4001; al-Dārimī in *al-Sunan*, vol. 2, p. 69 §1850; and Ibn Abī Shayba in *al-Muṣannaf*, vol. 3, p. 336 §14705.

> like the sanctity of this holy month and this holy land of yours.[1]

On the concept of human equality he stated:

«اَلنَّاسُ بَنُو آدَمَ، وَخَلَقَ اللهُ آدَمَ مِنْ تُرَابٍ».

> All mankind is the progeny of Adam and Allah created Adam from clay.[2]

Furthermore, he stated:

«يَا أَيُّهَا النَّاسُ! أَلَا إِنَّ رَبَّكُمْ وَاحِدٌ، وَإِنَّ أَبَاكُمْ وَاحِدٌ، أَلَا! لَا فَضْلَ لِعَرَبِيٍّ عَلَى أَعْجَمِيٍّ، وَلَا لِعَجَمِيٍّ عَلَى عَرَبِيٍّ، وَلَا لِأَحْمَرَ عَلَى أَسْوَدَ، وَلَا أَسْوَدَ عَلَى أَحْمَرَ إِلَّا بِالتَّقْوَى».

> O People! Be aware! Indeed your Lord is One and your father is one. Be aware! No Arab is superior to a non-Arab, and no non-Arab is superior to an Arab; no red person has a superiority over a black person, and no black person has superiority over a red person, except for those who are God-fearing.[3]

The Qur'ān clarifies this concept in these words:

﴿يَـٰٓأَيُّهَا ٱلنَّاسُ إِنَّا خَلَقْنَـٰكُم مِّن ذَكَرٍ وَأُنثَىٰ وَجَعَلْنَـٰكُمْ

---

[1] Related by Muslim in *al-Ṣaḥīḥ*, vol. 2, p. 889 §1218; Abū Dāwūd in *al-Sunan*, vol. 2, p. 185 §1905; Ibn Ḥibbān in *al-Ṣaḥīḥ*, vol. 9, .p. 257 §3944; al-Nasā'ī in *al-Sunan*, vo. 2, p. 421 §4001; al-Dārimī in *al-Sunan*, vol. 2, p. 69 §1850; and Ibn Abī Shayba in *al-Muṣannaf*, vol. 3, p. 336 §14705.

[2] Related by al-Tirmidhī in *al-Sunan*, vol. 5, p. 389 §3270; and al-Bayhaqī in *Shuʿab al-Īmān*, vol. 4, p. 286 §5130.

[3] Related by Aḥmad b. Ḥanbal in *al-Musnad*, vol. 5, p. 411; Ibn al-Mubārak in *al-Musnad*, p. 147 §239; and Haythamī in *Majmaʿ al-Zawā'id*, vol. 3, p. 266.

شُعُوبًا وَقَبَآئِلَ لِتَعَارَفُوٓاْۚ إِنَّ أَكۡرَمَكُمۡ عِندَ ٱللَّهِ أَتۡقَىٰكُمۡۚ إِنَّ ٱللَّهَ عَلِيمٌ خَبِيرٌ﴾

O people! We created you from a male and a female, and (divided) you into (large) peoples and tribes, so that you might recognize one another. Surely the most honourable among you in the sight of Allah is he who fears Allah most. Certainly Allah is All-Knowing, All-Aware.[1]

The Prophet Muhammad ﷺ abolished all falsely concocted superiorities and established the superiority of good character and mindfulness to God. His teachings eradicated economic exploitation and at the same time established the rights of women and the poor. Women were not only granted the right to vote but were also encouraged to take an active role within parliament. In the West, women were not politically enfranchised until the 20th century: it was not until 1920 that women were legally allowed to vote after the 19th Amendment was passed in America;[2] women were not declared as legal persons until 1929 in Canada. Women had to gain their legal rights gradually in the modern world and Western women have only enjoyed these rights for less than 100 years, whilst Islam provided women with rights instantly without any need of demonstration on their part 1400 hundred years ago.

In the days of the Caliph ʿUmar b. al-Khaṭṭāb ؓ, a motion was being discussed which limited the amount a women could receive in dower. During this discussion a women stood up

---

[1] Qurʾān 49: 13.

[2] Hart, James, The American Presidency in Action 1789: A Study in Constitutional History, New York, The Macmillan Company, 1948; Melvin I. Urofsky, Paul Finkelman, A March of Liberty: A Constitutional History of the United States (two volumes), Oxford University Press, 2002.

and criticised the bill, objecting that God did not limit the dower so why should ʿUmar; when asked for evidence for her claims she recited the following Qurʾānic verse:

﴿وَإِنْ أَرَدتُّمُ ٱسْتِبْدَالَ زَوْجٍ مَّكَانَ زَوْجٍ وَءَاتَيْتُمْ إِحْدَىٰهُنَّ
قِنطَارًا فَلَا تَأْخُذُوا۟ مِنْهُ شَيْـًٔا ۚ أَتَأْخُذُونَهُۥ بُهْتَـٰنًا وَإِثْمًا مُّبِينًا﴾

﴾And if you seek to take a wife in place of another and you have (by now) given to her heaps of wealth, yet do not take back any part of it. Do you want to take that wealth (back) by means of unjust accusation and manifest sin?﴿[1]

The objection of the woman suggests that she was a member of the parliament and therefore had both legal and political rights. When ʿUmar ؓ heard this evidence he quickly withdrew his bill and stated that the woman was correct and he was wrong.[2]

At the practical level, democracy was revived by the Prophet Muhammad ﷺ who established local governance in Medina. He organised a society in which a group of ten people was represented by a councillor known as an *ʿārif*, and a group of ten *ʿārifs* was represented by a deputy known as the *naqīb*; the *naqīb* was a member of the parliament in Medina. So every 100 persons in society were represented in parliament by their *naqīb*. Despite being the representative of God on earth, Prophet Muhammad ﷺ transferred power to the common member of society; this was a practical demonstration of consultative democracy in the life of the Prophet which characterised true Islamic societies.

If we are to revive peace in our world today we have to revive

---

[1] Qurʾān 4:20.

[2] Related by ʿAbd al-Razzāq in *al-Muṣannaf*, vol. 6, p. 180 §10420; and al-Shawkānī in *Nayl al-Awṭār*, vol. 6, p. 314.

the concept of multiculturalism; we must accept diversity in the world and not expect others to be subjected to our own criteria and customs. As demonstrated by the aforementioned evidences, returning to Islam is the only true viable means of achieving peace, as it champions the rights of every nation and enjoins multiculturalism and diversity.

2.4 A Detailed Exposition of the Meanings of Jihad: A Refutation of Misinterpretations

Another important aspect of Islam which has been manipulated is the concept of jihad and the misconceptions surrounding it need to be removed. This term has become popular amongst Muslims and non-Muslims alike but unfortunately it is confronted with misunderstandings on both sides. The word *jihād* comes from the word *juhd* which means 'to struggle';[1] it does not denote killing or warfare. It is a struggle for a greater good, for the betterment of mankind; it is a tool of eliminating oppression and terror; it is a means to an end, not an end within itself. The ultimate end of *jihād* is the establishment of peace at all levels. It is interesting to note that *jihād* is not monolithic: it is of various kinds and categories. The best *jihād*, and the greatest *jihād* in status, is *jihād bi'n-nafs*: to struggle against one's ego.

The Holy Prophet ﷺ said:

«الْـمُجَاهِدُ مَنْ جَاهَدَ نَفْسَهُ».

> The (great) striver is the one who strives against his own self (i.e., lusts, indulgences and luxurious

[1] Ibn Fāras, *Muʿjam Maqāyīs al-Lugha*, p. 210; Abū Manṣūr al-Azhārī, *Tahdhīb al-Lugha*, vol. 6, p. 26, Rāghib al-Aṣfahānī, *al-Mufradāt*, p. 101; Ibn Manẓūr, *Lisān al-ʿArab*, vol. 3, p. 143.

pursuits).[1]

After returning from a battle with his Companions, the Prophet stated:

«قَدِمْتُمْ مِنَ الْجِهَادِ الْأَصْغَرِ إِلَى الْجِهَادِ الْأَكْبَرِ».

> You have returned from a lesser (*al-jihād al-aṣghar*) to a supreme jihad (*al-jihād al-akbar*).[2]

The struggle against the self is a means of disciplining one's ego from evil propensities, such as sexual desires, material greed, lust for power and all other impure wishes. Islam does not aim to eliminate these completely but through self-discipline it aims to bring them under control; in this way Islam provides a means to organise one's life appropriately. This process of disciplining the soul is known as *tazkiya*, self-purification, which can be achieved through constant remembrance of Almighty Allah.

In Medina the Prophet used to provide an atmosphere for the Companions for the supreme jihad by conducting gatherings of Allah's remembrance for the purification of the soul.

The second jihad is *jihād bi'l-ʿilm*: the struggle for attaining and propagating knowledge. The Prophet told his Companions that if he were to choose between a group of people engaged in the remembrance of Allah and the other in the propagation of knowledge, he would choose the group

---

[1] Related by al-Tirmidhī in *al-Sunan*, vol. 4, p. 165 §1621; Ibn Ḥibbān in *al-Ṣaḥīḥ*, vol. 10, p. 484 §4624; al-Ḥākim in *al-Mustadrak*, vol. 2, p. 156 §2637; al-Bazzār in *al-Musnad*, vol. 2, p. 156 §3753; and al-Ṭabarānī in *al-Muʿjam al-Kabīr*, vol. 18, p. 256 §641.

[2] Related by al-Khaṭīb al-Baghdādī, in *Tārīkh Baghdād*, vol. 13, p. 523; Ibn ʿAsākir in *Tārīkh Dimashq al-Kabīr*, vol. 6, p. 438; Ibn Rajab al-Ḥanbalī in *Jāmiʿ al-ʿUlūm wa al- ikam*, vol. 1, p. 196; and al-Mizzī in *Tahdhīb al-Kamāl*, vol. 2, p. 144.

engaged in the attainment of knowledge. Thus the remembrance of Allah and the seeking of knowledge are declared the highest forms of jihad in Islam. This is why the first revelation of Islam was a revelation concerning the acquisition of knowledge. The Qur'ān states:

﴿ٱقْرَأْ بِٱسْمِ رَبِّكَ ٱلَّذِى خَلَقَ ۝١ خَلَقَ ٱلْإِنسَٰنَ مِنْ عَلَقٍ ۝٢ ٱقْرَأْ وَرَبُّكَ ٱلْأَكْرَمُ ۝٣ ٱلَّذِى عَلَّمَ بِٱلْقَلَمِ ۝٤ عَلَّمَ ٱلْإِنسَٰنَ مَا لَمْ يَعْلَمْ﴾

﴾(O Beloved!) Read (commencing) with the Name of Allah, Who has created (everything). He created man from a hanging mass (clinging) like a leech (in the mother's womb). Read and your Lord is Most Generous, Who taught man (reading and writing) by the pen, Who (besides that) taught man (all that) which he did not know.﴿[1]

Likewise, propagating the religion and calling others to the way of Islam is also a jihad which is known as *al-daʿwa*.

Jihād bi'l-ʿaml is the third kind of jihad which encourages people to do righteous deeds for the uplifting of morality; that you struggle for the promotion of spirituality, and guarding human values for society's betterment.

The fourth is *jihād bi'l-māl*: it is the jihad of charity that one spends their money to help the poor and needy.

Finally, the last kind of jihad is *jihād bi'l-qitāl*, which is the jihad of just-war (war for self-defence). After knowing this, it would be unjust to concentrate on this form of jihad at the exclusion of the rest. Furthermore, for this jihad to take place there are strict criteria and conditions. It was essentially legislated for the defence of one's rights, to defend humanity

[1] Qur'ān 96:1–5.

from all forms of oppression and aggression in the same way that the UN permits countries to wage war in self-defence.

Interestingly, *jihād bi'l-qitāl* was never commanded in the first nineteen years of the promulgation of Islam. The Prophet spent thirteen years in Mecca and was never commanded to fight. In Medina there was no commandment for *jihād bi'l-qitāl* for the first six years; whatever warfare was conducted in that time was purely committed out of self-defence and were fought near the boundaries of Medina. It was not until after the treaty of Ḥudaybiya that the Muslims were permitted to wage an offensive war against the enemies of humanity and mankind to eliminate terrorism and oppression. Almost two decades were spent in either peaceful preaching or self-defence until defensive warfare, *jihād bi'l-qitāl*, was permitted for Muslims. The Qur'ān states:

﴿أُذِنَ لِلَّذِينَ يُقَٰتَلُونَ بِأَنَّهُمْ ظُلِمُواْ وَإِنَّ ٱللَّهَ عَلَىٰ نَصْرِهِمْ لَقَدِيرٌ﴾

﴿Permission (to fight against mischief, disruption and oppression) is granted to those against whom (unjust) war is waged, because they were oppressed and Allah is doubtlessly All-Powerful to help them (the oppressed).﴾[1]

It is important to understand that *jihād bi'l-qitāl* is based on the concept of peace and is only permitted when all other forms of reconciliations have failed. Islam forbids one to either kill or maim any noncombatant;[2] doing so is considered a war crime. During warfare one is not allowed to kill or wound

[1] Qur'ān 22:39.

[2] Related by Muslim in *al-Ṣaḥīḥ*, vol. 3, p. 1407 §1780; Abū Dāwūd in *al-Sunan*, vol. 3, p. 162 §3021; and al-Bazzār in *al-Musnad*, vol. 4, p. 122 §1292.

worshippers who may be residing within a monastery or place of worship. Buildings and trees cannot be destroyed; and any kind of disturbances for the local population is totally forbidden.[1] Engaging in a conflict that contradicts any of these conditions would nullify the just cause of one's struggle, and one would be sinful in the eyes of God, as the purpose of *jihād bi'l-qitāl* is to bring about peace.

The Prophet's Companion and the first Rightly Guided Caliph Abū Bakr ﵁ would issue written and verbal instructions to the Muslim army to honour the above injunctions during a war.[2]

The notion that Islam was spread by the sword is false; Islam was spread peacefully through the integrity of its character and teachings, as attested by Phillip K. Hitti in his *History of the Arabs*. It is strange that today amongst the Muslims there is an unrestrained zeal to declare war against 'infidels' by misusing and abusing the term jihad. Such people have no understanding of what jihad means, instead they are fuelled by their egos and desires. They have no commitment to keeping to the strict guidelines set by our pious predecessors. As a result they create a greater loss and damage for Muslims, thereby exacerbating the problems that already exist.

It is a well-known principle that if there is clear indication that if going into conflict, one's enemy will become triumphant

---

[1] Related by Aḥmad b. Ḥanbal in *al-Musnad*, vol. 5, p. 385 §2728; Ibn Abī Shayba in *al-Muṣannaf*, vol. 6, pp. 483, 484 §33127, 33132; Abū Yaʿlā in *al-Musnad*, vol. 5, p. 59 §2650; al-Ṭaḥāwī in *Sharḥ Maʿānī al-Āthār*, vol. 3, p. 225; al-Bayhaqī in *al-Sunan al-Kubrā*, vol. 9, pp. 85, 90 §17904, 17929; and al-Daylamī in *Musnad al-Firdaws*, vol. 5, p. 45 §7410.

[2] Related by al-Tirmidhī in *al-Sunan*, vol. 4, p. 122 §1552; Mālik in *al-Mawaṭṭā*, vol. 2, p. 447 §965; ʿAbd al-Razzāq in *al-Muṣannaf*, vol. 5, p. 199 §9375; Ibn Abī Shayba in *al-Muṣannaf*, vol. 6, p. 483 §33121; al-Bayhaqī in *al-Sunan al-Kubrā*, vol. 9, pp. 89, 90 §17927, 17929; and al-Marwazī in *Musnad Abī Bakr*, pp. 69–72 §21.

or there is a great danger that irreparable damage will be inflicted on the Muslims, then going to war is prohibited. *Islam* discourages the believers from entering into a battle with their enemy if they are not adequately equipped. One tradition narrates that a group of Companions of the Prophet Muhammad ﷺ went to war. Upon realising that they were outnumbered and knowing that if they advanced towards their enemy they would face defeat, they retreated back to Medina. They informed the Prophet ﷺ, telling him, '*naḥnu al-farrārūn, yā Rasūl Allāh*', 'We are ones who fled (from the battlefield) O Messenger of Allah.' The Prophet ﷺ replied, '*lā, bal antum al-ʿakkārūn*', 'No, in fact you are the ones who returned safely.'[1] Through these words they were consoled.

This shows that if one advances to war and there is a chance of irreparable loss and damage, then fighting no longer becomes obligatory, but prohibited, and it becomes necessary to avoid fighting in order to curb the possibility of long-term damage. How far are the cries of those people who call for jihad in the modern world from the noble practice of our ancestors.

2.5 Historic Existence of Extremists and Terrorists in the Form of the Kharijite

Within the Muslim community where a minority has left the path of balance and moderation, the duty is upon the majority to reclaim the beautiful religion of Islam from the extremists; we cannot allow them to speak in our name. The extremists have adopted a twofold strategy to target the youth: intellectually and militantly. The former is related to the Zahirite ideology, whilst the latter is related to the Kharijites. The Muslim youths

[1] Related by Abū Dāwūd in *al-Sunan*, vol. 3, p. 46 §2647; al-Tirmidhī in *al-Sunan*, vol. 4, p. 215 §1716; Aḥmad b. Ḥanbal in *al-Musnad*, vol. 2, pp. 70, 100, 110; and al-Bayhaqī in *al-Sunan al-Kubrā*, vol. 9, p. 76 §17861–17862.

must take great precaution for they are most vulnerable and most likely to be preyed upon. The Zahirite ideology has been absolutely rejected by the majority of Muslims throughout history: this ideology exacted a literalist interpretation of the Qur'ān and Sunna and they did not go beyond the letter of the law. In time they lost sight of the aims and objectives of the Shariah and had lost the spirit of the law. They sought to fulfil the legal rulings of the Shariah but neglected its wisdom, and so within time their school became inept and their influence was wiped away from Muslim societies.

The Zahirites went against the verse of the Qur'ān in which Allah states:

﴿وَيُعَلِّمُكُمُ ٱلْكِتَٰبَ وَٱلْحِكْمَةَ﴾

﴾And he teaches you the Book and inculcates in you logic and wisdom.﴿[1]

Understanding the wisdom behind the text is paramount for the correct application of the Shariah in the world. In matters of worship and spirituality the rulings remain predominantly the same, but as for matters concerning the secular aspect of one's life there is a need to understand the wisdom behind the rulings, because as things change and new situations arise the rulings change in order to make the Shariah fully adept to the environment in which it is practiced; and, as we have seen, the Zahirite ideology which refused to adapt and reconstruct itself became outmoded and unfit for society; it lost adherents and became extinct. This dynamic spirit of reconstruction is the concept of *ijtihād*, which vitalises the spirit of the Shariah making it practicable in every age and society. This is what a qualified *mujtahid* does: he interprets the texts and applies it appropriately according to the dictates of time and place. In no way does this mean that the Shariah is subjugated to the

---

[1] Qur'ān 2:151.

whims and fancies of men, but rather the *mujtahid* who seeks to apply the spirit of the Shariah earnestly strives to stay true to the letter of the law to the best of his ability. Thus Islam in this sense is not a static and outmoded religion, but rather it is dynamic.

As for the Kharijites, Muslim history bears testimony to their unorthodoxy and heresy. They were declared as outcasts by the Prophet and the Rightly Guided Caliphs. In fact they *fought* against the fourth Rightly Guided Caliph, ʿAlī al-Murtaḍā ؉. They were narrow-minded and possessed a short-sighted understanding of their religion and life in general. Their hallmark was that they were equipped with the best slogans and had a tendency to declare others as disbelievers and infidels. They were the most vocal for the implementation of the Shariah and for establishing God's rule on earth; so when ʿAlī, the fourth Rightly Guided Caliph of Islam, accepted mediation during the battle of Ṣiffīn, the Kharijites were quick to condemn him for what they believed was a compromise of God's rule and declared him an infidel.[1] Their slogan was *ini'l-ḥukm illā li-Allāh*: 'there is no rule except for God's.' ʿAlī al-Murtaḍā ؉, when asked about this slogan, replied:

«كَلِمَةُ حَقٍّ أُرِيْدَ بِهَا بَاطِلٌ».

That is true but the intentions behind it are invalid.[2]

We can see the remnants of the Kharijite legacy amongst the youths who have become frustrated with the frequent mishaps in the Muslim world. As a result of perceived attacks

---

[1] For complete details, see: Qadri, Tahir-ul., *Fatwa on Terrorism and Suicide Bombings*. United Kingdom: Bodmin and King's Lynn, 2010.

[2] Related by Muslim in *al-Ṣaḥīḥ*, vol. 2, p. 749 §1066; al-Nasāʾī in *al-Sunan al-Kubrā*, vol. 5, p. 160 §8562; Ibn Abī Shayba in *al-Muṣannaf*, vol. 7, p. 557 §37907; and al-Bayhaqī in *al-Sunan al-Kubrā*, vol. 8, p.171 §16478.

against their Islamic identity, they vent their anger through the extremist groups who they feel are the only ones addressing their concerns. Their slogans such as Shariah for the UK, behead those who insult Islam, jihad is our way, freedom of speech go to hell, are all manifestations of this Kharijite tendency that has re-emerged amongst young Muslims due to their emotional frustration. However this minority possesses no legitimate religious authority and is completely alien to the teachings and wisdoms of Islam.

2.6 Prophetic Biography (*Sīra*) as a Model for the Umma's Success

For the Muslims, success will now only emerge if they retract to the *sīra* of the Prophet Muhammad ﷺ. His life can be divided into three stages: the first stage in Mecca and two significant stages in Medina.

The Prophet ﷺ spent the first thirteen years of his life in Mecca, teaching the early Muslims about strengthening one's faith and building upon one's morality, ethics and spirituality. Through the firmness of faith, Islam was spread, this period was therefore characterised with the advancement of knowledge. Thereafter the Prophet ﷺ migrated to Medina and this migration heralded the second phase. In the six or seven years of the first Medinan phase there was a greater concentration upon the building of the Muslim state. Its initiation was characterised by a social contract known as the *muwākhāt*, which brought together warring tribes under a unified banner. During these years efforts were made for the social and economic stability of the newly formed community: steps were taken by the Prophet ﷺ for the elimination of poverty in order to grant the citizens of the society with economic stability and prosperity; he made all Muslim brothers to one another and distributed their wealth amongst them so that all economic deadlocks may be resolved; they would share their earnings and holdings so that they would become economically strong to stave off any potential threat or enemy.

As a result of the Constitution of Medina Prophet Muhammad ﷺ created peace between the various tribes and also brought the Jewish tribes into the treaty. The Jews were fully integrated into the Muslim community. However, with the passage of time, as the Muslims gained both economic and political strength the Jews broke off their alliance. During these six years, it was clear that relations between the Jews and Muslims would not last; Allah informed the Muslims in the Qur'ān about their hostility, but the Prophet ﷺ did not fight against them lest he would be confronted by two powerful enemies at the same time: the polytheist of Mecca in the south and the Jews of Khybar in the north. And indeed the Muslims were attacked.

The Prophet ﷺ knew of these developments so he set out to Mecca with his Companions ﷺ for the Hajj pilgrimage. When the Meccans prevented him and his followers from entering the city he signed a ten-year no-war pact which historically became known as the 'Treaty of Ḥudaybiyya.' The Treaty of Ḥudaybiyya marked the beginning of the third phase of the *sīra* of the Prophet ﷺ: As a result of the treaty he, through his wisdom, prevented his enemies from attacking him from the south whilst he dealt with his enemies from the north; by doing so he avoided the Muslims from fighting a double fronted battle. At the time of signing the treaty the Companions were not aware of its inherent wisdom: the majority of the clauses were actually not in favour of the Muslims and were heavily biased towards the Meccans, giving them privileges at the expense of the Muslims. But despite the unevenness of this treaty, the Prophet ﷺ signed it and told the companions to be patient for it heralded a truly great victory.

Being barred from entry into Mecca and not being allowed to perform Ḥajj that year, the Holy Prophet ﷺ ordered the

Companions ﷺ to get ready for a pre-emptive attack. With the polytheists bound from the south the Muslims were safe to dispose of their enemies in the north; the result was a decisive victory for the Muslims: Khybar had been conquered. This victory turned the tide and made Islam the most powerful force in the Arabian Peninsula.

For nineteen years the Holy Prophet ﷺ and the Muslims remained patient with their enemies: the first thirteen years were characterised by non-violence and non-retaliation whilst the latter six years were of self-defence.

2.7 Closing Words: The True Way Forward for Muslims

So what steps should we take? First and foremost Muslims must strengthen themselves spiritually, morally and ethically; they must revive the culture of learning and academia and strengthen themselves technologically and scientifically. Then, following the precedent of the Holy Prophet ﷺ in Medina, the Muslim world should strengthen itself economically and bring together its resources in a way similar to the EU which began its journey from a European 'economic community' to the 'European Union'. The Muslim world cannot be revived politically unless it alleviates poverty and bears in mind that this current unipolar world is an unstable one and that a multipolar world is bound to emerge. The next poles of global polar will be Europe, Russia, and the South Pacific Rim including China and Japan. The Muslim world consists of fifty-six countries and can become a power bloc if it has the will, but only if it strengthens itself both scientifically and technologically. Once consolidated, it will have the power to choose who it wishes to aligns itself with: Europe, Russia, or the South Pacific Rim; and it can then ultimately present itself as an equal in the world.

Part Three A

Islam, Peace and Democracy

Islam is a religion of peace and democracy; it is my intention to explore this aspect of Islam using Islam's first written constitution. It was drafted by the Holy Prophet Muhammad ﷺ when he was declared head of the state of Medina.

3.1 Etymology of the Arabic Word Islam

Let us start by exploring the root word of Islam. The root word of Islam is *silm* and *salama*, which means to come into peace and to provide others with peace.[1]

The Qur'ān states:

﴿يَـٰٓأَيُّهَا ٱلَّذِينَ ءَامَنُوا۟ ٱدْخُلُوا۟ فِى ٱلسِّلْمِ كَآفَّةً﴾

﴿*O believers! Enter Islam perfectly and wholly.*﴾[2]

Any act, policy, or stance which is against the peace of mankind is considered an un-Islamic activity. This concept of Islam was practiced and propagated by the Holy Prophet Muhammad ﷺ. In order to elucidate this concept further, I would like to present the life of the Holy Prophet Muhammad ﷺ as an archetype which will serve as a practical demonstration and an exegesis of Allah's commandment of adopting peace in its entirety.

---

[1] Ibn Manẓūr, *Lisān al-ʿArab*, vol. 12, p. 289; Rāghib al-Aṣfahānī, *al-Mufradāt*, pp. 239, 240.

[2] Qurʾān 2:208.

3.2 Seven-Point Social Policy Formulated by the Holy Prophet ﷺ

Before the Prophet ﷺ decided to emigrate from Mecca to Medina, a gathering took place in Minā (near Mecca). The gathering formed what was to be known as the first pledge of allegiance; the *bayʿa al-ʿaqaba al-ʾūlā*. Twelve people from Medina came to see the Holy Prophet Muhammad ﷺ and embraced Islam. Thereafter they made a hand-in-hand pledge with the Holy Prophet ﷺ, affirming their loyalty and allegiance to him. During this meeting, the Prophet ﷺ delivered a sermon and introduced Islam to them which was to be their very first lesson on the religion. Later, the twelve delegates were appointed by the Holy Prophet ﷺ as his representatives; to propagate and introduce Islam to the society of Medina.[1]

This first sermon consisted of seven points, and through these points the Prophet ﷺ laid down his vision of a good society. The first point of this sermon was a commandment of faith and obedience to Almighty Allah - the Lord and Creator. The second point, after belief in the creator and submission to Him, was the prohibition of theft. The third point was that there should be no adultery or fornication in one's life, so that one is free from all sexual immoralities and crimes. Fourth, there should be no killing, particularly of females and mankind in general. Fifth, there should be no false allegations or false accusations against anyone. Sixth, that there should be no back-biting. Finally, the seventh point was the obligation to practice and propagate the good and to abstain from evil. The delegate returned to Medina with this message of Islam. All basic books of Islamic history have narrated this sermon

---

[1] Related by al-Bukhārī in *al-Ṣaḥīḥ*, vol. 1, p. 15 §18; Aḥmad b. Ḥanbal in *al-Musnad*, vol. 5, p. 323; Ibn Hishām in *al-Sīra al-Nabawiyya*, vol. 6, p. 281; al-Ṭabarī in *Tārīkh al-Umam wa al-Mulūk*, vol. 1, p. 559; Ibn Kathīr in *al-Bidāya wa al-Nihāya*, vol. 3, pp. 150, 151; and Ibn Khaldūn in his well-known *History*, vol. 2, p. 348.

undisputedly. So this is not any isolated tradition, but a well-known and unanimously agreed-upon tradition.

Note, that only one point (out of the seven) is related to the religious and spiritual message of Islam. The rest are related to the reformation and refinement of man's moral ethics and conduct, and are all secular in nature. The Prophet's main emphasis was to protect human life in its individual sphere, as well as in its collective sphere, from all kinds of social crimes and injustices.

3.3 The First Public Friday Address Delivered by The Holy Prophet ﷺ to The People Of Medina

When the Holy Prophet ﷺ eventually migrated from Mecca to Medina, he delivered his first public Friday lecture in Masjid al-Jumʿa [Mosque], as recorded by the authorities of Islamic history.[1] This extended Friday lecture became his first official public address directed at the inhabitants of Medina. A point of note here is that although the Holy Prophet ﷺ was personally in great trouble and difficulty; forced to leave his beloved homeland Mecca due to the Meccans' oppression and cruelty towards him, he never once mentioned a single aspect of their misconduct towards him in his address. A diligent observer will recognise that the Prophet ﷺ came to Medina specifically determined in setting up a just and democratic society based on Islamic ideals and morals.

Like the sermon on the day of the first pledge of allegiance, the first sermon addressed to the citizens of Medina by the

---

[1] Related by al-Ṭabarī in *Tārīkh al-Umam wa al-Mulūk*, vol. 2, pp. 7, 8; Ibn al-Jawzī in *al-Muntaẓam fī Tārīkh al-Mulūk wa al-Umam*, vol. 3, pp. 65–67; al-Qurṭubī in *al-Jāmiʿ li-Aḥkām al-Qurʾān*, vol. 18, pp. 98–100; and Ibn Kathīr in *al-Bidāya wa al-Nihāya*, vol. 3, pp. 212–214.

Holy Prophet ﷺ, was the lesson of worship and obedience to Almighty Allah. In it he also emphasised truthfulness and mutual love amongst everyone, to fulfil promises and commitments, and finally to differentiate and discriminate between the lawful and unlawful in one's life with piety and God-wariness, so that nobody is harmed by one's actions and conduct. Again, the whole of this lecture consisted of a policy of social reform; a policy based on human rights, human dignity, and mutual brotherhood.

3.4 Brief Examination of the Constitution Delivered by the Holy Prophet ﷺ

After briefly glossing over these two sermons of the Holy Prophet ﷺ, I would like to turn your attention to a constitution gifted to humanity by the Holy Prophet ﷺ, which was known as *al-Ṣaḥīfa*, or the 'Constitution of Medina'. This constitution brought within its jurisdictions the local Muslim inhabitants of Medina, the emigrants of Mecca, the local Jewish community and other non-Muslim tribes, as well as their allies. The constitution delineated the constitutional foundation of the Medinan society; it provided the concept of devolution of powers which materialised into democracy in the practical sense. Through the constitution, a moderate and balanced aptitude was formulated towards all communities regardless of their faith or ethnicity. The concept of a unified geographical and territorial nation, which includes Muslims and non-Muslims alike and which brought together various faiths and cultures, was advanced by the Holy Prophet ﷺ. Likewise, the supremacy of the rule of law was also articulated through the constitution coupled with respect for local customs and laws. The tradition of all local tribes under the rule of law, and protection of culture and religion was advocated. Through the constitution, the Holy Prophet ﷺ postulated basic human rights thereby introducing the concept of protection of religious freedom of minorities, and the protection of their culture and religion. The Holy Prophet ﷺ declared the state of Medina as a sanctuary of peace and security; no act of oppression, injustice, or extremism would be allowed in the state of Medina.

The constitution begins with the Holy Prophet ﷺ declaring the Muslims and Jews, a single nation. In this declaration he did not exclude non-Muslims from being part of the Medinan community, as he was unanimously accepted as the head of state.

3.4.1 Opening Articles

Article 1 states:

«هَذَا كِتَابٌ مِنْ مُحَمَّدٍ النَّبِيِّ (رَسُولُ الله)».

> This is a (constitutional) document from Muhammad the Prophet (and Messenger of Allah for the nations of the world).[1]

The subsequent article, states:

«بَيْنَ الْـمُؤْمِنِينَ وَالْـمُسْلِمِينَ مِنْ قُرَيْشٍ وَ(أَهْلِ) يَثْرِب، وَمَنْ تَبِعَهُمْ فَلَحِقَ بِهِمْ وَجَاهَدَ مَعَهُمْ».

> This compact has been concluded between the believers and Muslims of Quraysh and Yathrib, and those who, in compliance, later, join their (political) alliance to fight the defensive war together.[2]

---

[1] Related by Ibn Hishām in *al-Sīra al-Nabawiyya*, vol. 3, p. 31; Abū ʿUbayd al-Qāsim in *Kitāb al-Amwāl*, vol. 1, p. 260; Ibn Zanjuway in *Kitāb al-Amwāl*, p. 205; Ibn Taymiyya in *al-Ṣārim al-Maslūl*, p. 62; Ibn Kathīr in *al-Bidāya wa al-Nihāya*, vol. 2, p. 260; Ibn Sayyid al-Nās in *ʿUyūn al-Athar*, vol. 1, p. 227; and al-Ṣāliḥī in *Subul al-Hudā wa al-Rishād*, vol. 3, p. 382.

[2] Related by Ibn Hishām in *al-Sīra al-Nabawiyya*, vol. 3, p. 32; Abū

And, article 3 confirms:

«إِنَّهُمْ أُمَّةٌ وَاحِدَةٌ مِنْ دُونِ النَّاسِ».

> (Owing to this unique alliance) a single community (political union) comprising all (the contracting parties to the compact) has emerged to the exclusion of all the peoples of the world.[1]

The constitution's opening articles state that Muslims of Quraysh and Yathrib, and those who followed and joined them, are of one community. The policies of the new Medinan State assert that the immigrant Muslims of Mecca and native Muslims of Medina constitute one community. The constitution established a free Islamic State on the principles of equality, equity, and religious freedom.

3.4.2 FREEDOM OF RELIGION

An entire chapter of the Qur'ān which guarantees man's religious freedom even if it is contrary to Muslim beliefs demonstrates the highest possible form of religious tolerance.

ʿUbayd al-Qāsim in *Kitāb al-Amwāl*, vol. 1, p. 260; Ibn Zanjuway in *Kitāb al-Amwāl*, p. 205; al-Bayhaqī in *al-Sunan al-Kubrā*, vol. 8, p. 106; Ibn Taymiyya in *al-Ṣārim al-Maṣlūl*, p. 62; Ibn al-Qayyim in *Aḥkām Ahl al-Dhimma*, vol. 3, p. 1405; Ibn Kathīr in *al-Bidāya wa al-Nihāya*, vol. 2, p. 260; Ibn Sayyid al-Nās in *ʿUyūn al-Athar*, vol. 1, p. 227; al-Suhaylī in *al-Rawḍ al-Unuf*, vol. 2, p. 349; and al-Ṣāliḥī in *Subul al-Hudā wa al-Rishād*, vol. 3, p. 382.

[1] Related by Ibn Hishām in *al-Sīra al-Nabawiyya*, vol. 3, p. 32; Abū ʿUbayd al-Qāsim in *Kitāb al-Amwāl*, vol. 1, p. 260; Ibn Zanjuway in *Kitāb al-Amwāl*, p. 205; al-Bayhaqī in *al-Sunan al-Kubrā*, vol. 8, p. 106; Ibn Taymiyya in *al-Ṣārim al-Maslūl*, p. 63; Ibn al-Qayyim in *Aḥkām Ahl al-Dhimma*, vol. 3, p. 1405; Ibn Kathīr in *al-Bidāya wa al-Nihāya*, vol. 2, p. 260; Ibn Sayyid al-Nās in *ʿUyūn al-Athar*, vol. 1, p. 227; al-Suhaylī in *al-Rawḍ al-Unuf*, vol. 2, p. 349; and al-Ṣāliḥī in *Subul al-Hudā wa al-Rishād*, vol. 3, p. 382.

The Qurʾān states in the chapter of *al-Kāfirūn* (the disbelievers):

﴿قُلْ يَـٰٓأَيُّهَا ٱلْكَـٰفِرُونَ ۝١ لَآ أَعْبُدُ مَا تَعْبُدُونَ ۝٢ وَلَآ أَنتُمْ عَـٰبِدُونَ مَآ أَعْبُدُ ۝٣ وَلَآ أَنَا۠ عَابِدٌ مَّا عَبَدتُّمْ ۝٤ وَلَآ أَنتُمْ عَـٰبِدُونَ مَآ أَعْبُدُ ۝٥ لَكُمْ دِينُكُمْ وَلِىَ دِينِ﴾

﴿*Say: 'O disbelievers! I do not worship that which you worship. Nor do you worship Whom I worship. And I shall never worship that which you worship. Nor will you worship Whom I worship. (So) you have your* dīn *(religion), and I have my* Dīn *(Religion).'*﴾[1]

This constitution further substantiates this point in article thirty stating:

«وَإِنَّ يَهُودَ بَنِي عَوْفٍ أُمَّةٌ مَعَ الْـمُؤْمِنِينَ لِلْيَهُودِ دِينُهُمْ وَلِلْمُسْلِمِينَ دِينُهُمْ».

The Jews of the Banū ʿAwf are one community (political union) with the believers. The Jews have their religion and the Muslims and their associates have theirs, except those who behave unjustly and sinfully, for they hurt but themselves and their families.[2]

---

[1] Qurʾān 109:1–6.

[2] Related by Ibn Hishām in *al-Sīra al-Nabawiyya*, vol. 3, p. 34; Abū ʿUbayd al-Qāsim in *Kitāb al-Amwāl*, vol. 1, p. 263; Ibn Zanjuway in *Kitāb al-Amwāl*, p. 392; Ibn Taymiyya in *al-Ṣārim al-Maslūl*, p. 63; Ibn al-Qayyim in *Aḥkām Ahl al-Dhimma*, vol. 3, p. 1407; Ibn Kathīr in *al-Bidāya wa al-Nihāya*, vol. 2, p. 261; Ibn Sayyid al-Nās, vol. 1, p. 228; al-Suhaylī in *al-Rawḍ al-Unuf*, vol. 2, p. 349; and al-Ṣāliḥī in *Subul al-Hudā wa al-Rishād*, vol. 3, p. 382.

From article thirty to forty the Holy Prophet ﷺ mentioned each and every Jewish tribe specifically by name, guaranteeing them their right of protection under the new Constitution.

The Qur'ān also states:

﴿لَآ إِكۡرَاهَ فِي ٱلدِّينِۖ﴾

﴾*There is no compulsion in* Dīn *(Religion).*﴿[1]

There can be no narrowness in Islam, nor can there be any inconvenience. A Muslim cannot enforce hardship on another person or compel others to their way: forced conversions have no place in this pure religion. Compelling others to embrace Islam is against Islam and the teachings of the Qur'ān. Everybody has a right to practice his/her own religion; rather Islam has enjoined Muslim rulers to protect the places of worship of non-Muslims.

In the days of Banū Umayya (Omayyad Dynasty), Walīd b. ʿAbd al-Malik, one of the Umayyad governors, demolished a portion of a church in Damascus, and had extended a mosque in its stead. When the caliph ʿUmar b. ʿAbd al-ʿAzīz ؓ got the news, he ordered that the extended portion of the mosque be demolished and the church rebuilt, and it was done. The tradition says:

فَلَمَّا اسْتَخْلَفَ عُمَرُ بْنُ عَبْدِ الْعَزِيْزِ ؓ، شَكَى النَّصَارَى إِلَيْهِ مَا فَعَلَ الْوَلِيْدُ بِهِمْ فِي كَنِيْسَتِهِمْ، فَكَتَبَ إِلَى عَامِلِهِ يَأْمُرُهُ بِرَدِّ مَا زَادَهُ فِي الْـمَسْجِدِ.

When ʿUmar b. ʿAbd al-ʿAzīz ؓ took over as Caliph, the Christians complained to him about al-Walīd's forcible occupation of Church land. He ordered the official to get that part of the Mosque demolished,

---

[1] Qur'ān 2:256.

> which had been constructed on the land of Church, and return it to Christians. So the same was done.[1]

Freedom of expression, the rights of ill people and elderly citizens, the right of protection for one's property, and the right of forming contracts were all guaranteed under the new constitution.

3.4.3 Forbiddance of Bloodshed

The constitution forbade fighting and bloodshed amongst the various communities of the state:

«وَإِنَّ يَثْرِبَ حَرَامٌ جَوْفُهَا لِأَهْلِ هَذِهِ الصَّحِيفَةِ».

> The Yathrib valley (Medina, fenced by hills) shall be a sanctuary (the abode of peace) for the people of this document. (Here all mutual conflicts are prohibited.)[2]

Likewise, as stated in article sixty-one, any oppressor, militant, or tyrant that commits an act of cruelty, oppression or suppression is to be deprived of the protection given by the constitution:

«وَإِنَّهُ لَا يَحُولُ هَذَا الْكِتَابُ دُونَ ظَالِمٍ وَآثِمٍ».

> This document will not be employed to protect one who betrays, is unjust or violates the treaty.[3]

---

[1] Related by al-Balādhurī in *Futūḥ al-Buldān*, p. 150.

[2] Related by Ibn Hishām in *al-Sīra al-Nabawiyya*, vol. 3, p. 34; Abū ʿUbayd al-Qāsim in *Kitāb al-Amwāl*, vol. 1, p. 263; and Ibn Zanjuway in *Kitāb al-Amwāl*, p. 206.

[3] Related by Ibn Hishām in *al-Sīra al-Nabawiyya*, vol. 3, p. 35; Abū ʿUbayd al-Qāsim in *Kitāb al-Amwāl*, vol. 1, p. 263; Ibn Zanjuway in *Kitāb al-Amwāl*, p. 206; Ibn Sayyid al-Nās in *ʿUyūn al-Athar*, vol. 1, p. 228; al-Suhaylī in *al-Rawḍ al-Unuf*, vol. 2, p. 350; and al-Ṣāliḥī in *Subul al-Hudā wa al-Rishād*, vol. 3, p. 383.

Furthermore, in the penultimate article, sixty-two, the constitution states:

«وَإِنَّهُ مَنْ خَرَجَ آمِنٌ وَمَنْ قَعَدَ آمِنٌ بِالْـمَدِينَةِ إِلّا مَنْ ظَلَمَ أَوْ أَثِمَ».

> Whether an individual goes out to fight or remains in his home, he will be safe in Medina unless he has perpetrated injustice or violated law.[1]

Ultimately, the constitution guaranteed protection to peaceful citizens, whilst those people who worked against the peace and security of the state and its people, would lose their guaranteed constitutional protection for their life.

The final article sixty-three, states:

«وَإِنَّ اللهَ جَارٌ لِمَنْ بَرَّ وَاتَّقَى وَمُحَمَّدٌ رَسُولُ اللهِ».

> Allah along with His Messenger Muhammad is the Protector of those pious and God-fearing people who remain loyal and adherent to this (constitutional) document.[2]

3.4.4 PROTECTION OF HUMAN LIFE

Many of the fundamental human rights which we enjoy

---

[1] Related by Ibn Hishām in *al-Sīra al-Nabawiyya*, vol. 3, p. 35; Abū ʿUbayd al-Qāsim in *Kitāb al-Amwāl*, vol. 1, p. 263; Ibn Zanjuway in *Kitāb al-Amwāl*, p. 206; Ibn Sayyid al-Nās in *ʿUyūn al-Athar*, vol. 1, p. 229; al-Suhaylī in *al-Rawḍ al-Unuf*, vol. 2, p. 350; Ibn Kathīr in *al-Bidāya wa al-Nihāya*, vol. 2, p. 262; and al-Ṣāliḥī in *Subul al-Hudā wa al-Rishād*, vol. 3, p. 383.

[2] Related by Ibn Hishām in *al-Sīra al-Nabawiyya*, vol. 3, p. 35; Ibn Zanjuway in *Kitāb al-Amwāl*, p. 206; al-Suhaylī in *al-Rawḍ al-Unuf*, vol. 2, p. 350; and Ibn Kathīr in *al-Bidāya wa al-Nihāya*, vol. 2, p. 226.

today were declared by the Holy Prophet ﷺ through the Holy Qur'ān and his practice. The right to the protection of life was declared in chapter five of the Holy Qur'ān, verse thirty-two, in which Allah states:

﴿مَن قَتَلَ نَفْسًا بِغَيْرِ نَفْسٍ أَوْ فَسَادٍ فِي ٱلْأَرْضِ فَكَأَنَّمَا قَتَلَ ٱلنَّاسَ جَمِيعًا وَمَنْ أَحْيَاهَا فَكَأَنَّمَآ أَحْيَا ٱلنَّاسَ جَمِيعًا﴾

﴿Whoever killed a person (unjustly), except as a punishment for murder or for (spreading) disorder in the land, it would be as if he killed all the people (of society); and whoever (saved him from unjust murder and) made him survive, it would be as if he saved the lives of all the people (of society; i.e. he rescued the collective system of human life).﴾[1]

Therefore, the murder of any human being regardless of their religion, race or colour is forbidden in Islam and doing so amounts to the murder of humanity. Similarly, serving one person is equivalent to serving the whole of mankind.

In fact, those who are in the womb of their mothers have also been guaranteed this right to life; because the right to life is such a precious thing that nobody can act against it.

Mankind has been accorded with such respect and honour that even after his death, no one is permitted to abuse his deceased body, regardless whether he is a Muslim or not. Narrated by ʿĀ'isha ﵂:

قَالَ النَّبِيُّ ﷺ: «لَا تَسُبُّوا الْأَمْوَاتَ فَإِنَّهُمْ قَدْ أَفْضَوْا إِلَى مَا قَدَّمُوا».

The Prophet ﷺ said, 'Do not abuse the dead ones, because they have reached the result of what they

[1] Qur'ān 5:32.

forwarded.'[1]

It is narrated in an agreed upon tradition:

عَنْ جَابِرِ بْنِ عَبْدِ اللهِ ﷺ، قَالَ: مَرَّ بِنَا جِنَازَةٌ فَقَامَ لَهَا النَّبِيُّ ﷺ، وَقُمْنَا بِهِ، فَقُلْنَا: يَا رَسُولَ اللهِ! إِنَّهَا جِنَازَةٌ يَهُودِيٍّ. قَالَ ﷺ: «إِذَا رَأَيْتُمُ الْجِنَازَةَ فَقُومُوا».

Jābir b. 'Abd Allāh ☙ narrates: 'A funeral passed us by and the Prophet ﷺ stood up for it. We stood up, and then we said: O Messenger of Allah, it is a funeral of a Jew. The Prophet ﷺ replied: If you see a funeral stand.'[2]

Notice, when the Companions ☙ enquired about the Prophet's action and had informed him that the funeral passing by him was not that of a Muslim but a Jew; the Prophet ﷺ showed no concern for the religion or the culture of that person. Instead, he expressed his respect stating that the funerals of all people are to be respected, as this is a fundamental human right that transcends all divides.

Islam has accorded respect and honour to every man and woman in that nobody is allowed to insult or curse another. The Holy Prophet ﷺ has even prohibited the Muslims from

---

[1] Related by al-Bukhārī in *al-Ṣaḥīḥ*, vol. 1, p. 470 §1329; al-Nasā'ī in *al-Sunan*, vol. 4, p. 53 §1936; and *al-Sunan al-Kubrā*, vol. 1, p. 630 §2063; Ibn Ḥibbān in *al-Ṣaḥīḥ*, vol. 7, p. 291 §3021; Aḥmad b. Ḥanbal in *al-Musnad*, vol. 6, p. 180 §25509; al-Dārimī in *al-Sunan*, vol. 2, p. 311 §2511; al-Ḥākim in *al-Mustadrak*, vol. 1, p. 541 §419; and al-Bayhaqī in *al-Sunan al-Kubrā*, vol. 4, p. 75 §6979; and *Shu'ab al-Īmān*, vol. 5, p. 287 §6678.

[2] Related by al-Bukhārī in *al-Ṣaḥīḥ*, vol. 1, p. 441 §1249; Muslim in *al-Ṣaḥīḥ*, vol. 2, p. 660 §960; al-Nasā'ī in *al-Sunan*, vol. 4, p. 45 §1922; and *al-Sunan al-Kubrā*, vol. 1, p. 626 §2049; and Aḥmad b. Ḥanbal in *al-Musnad*, vol. 3, p. 319 §14467.

cursing or torturing animals and insects.

ʿAbd al-Raḥmān b. ʿAbd Allāh quoted his father as saying that once they were on a journey in the company of Allah's Messenger ﷺ and he had gone to relieve himself. The Companions ﵃ saw a sparrow with two young ones. When they took the young ones, the sparrow, greatly upset, came and began to spread out its wings. When the Holy Prophet ﷺ returned, he said:

«مَنْ فَجَعَ هَذِهِ بِوَلَدِهَا؟ رُدُّوا وَلَدَهَا إِلَيْهَا».

> Who has pained this one by the (loss of) her young ones? Give her young ones back to her.[1]

Then the Holy Prophet ﷺ saw an anthill, which had been burned. He declared such an act prohibited:

«إِنَّهُ لَا يَنْبَغِي أَنْ يُعَذِّبَ بِالنَّارِ إِلَّا رَبُّ النَّارِ».

> It is not fitting that anyone should punish with fire but the Lord of the fire.[2]

ʿAbd Allāh b. ʿUmar ﵄ narrated that Allah's Messenger ﷺ stated:

«عُذِّبَتِ امْرَأَةٌ فِي هِرَّةٍ حَبَسَتْهَا، حَتَّى مَاتَتْ جُوعًا، فَدَخَلَتْ فِيهَا النَّارَ». قَالَ: «فَقَالَ: وَاللهُ أَعْلَمُ، لَا أَنْتِ أَطْعَمْتِهَا وَلَا سَقَيْتِهَا حِينَ حَبَسْتِيهَا، وَلَا أَنْتِ أَرْسَلْتِهَا فَأَكَلَتْ مِنْ خَشَاشِ الْأَرْضِ».

> A woman was tortured and was put in Hell because of a cat which she had kept locked till it died of hunger. Allah's Messenger ﷺ further said, Allah knows better. Allah said (to the woman), 'You neither fed it

---

[1] Related by Abū Dāwūd in *al-Sunan*, vol. 3, p. 55 §2675.

[2] Related by Abū Dāwūd in *al-Sunan*, vol. 3, p. 55 §2675.

nor watered when you locked it up, nor did you set it free to eat the insects of the earth.'[1]

3.4.5 Right of Privacy

Likewise, Islam has given man the right of privacy. Allah states:

﴿يَـٰٓأَيُّهَا ٱلَّذِينَ ءَامَنُوا۟ لَا تَدْخُلُوا۟ بُيُوتًا غَيْرَ بُيُوتِكُمْ حَتَّىٰ تَسْتَأْنِسُوا۟ وَتُسَلِّمُوا۟ عَلَىٰٓ أَهْلِهَا ۚ ذَٰلِكُمْ خَيْرٌ لَّكُمْ لَعَلَّكُمْ تَذَكَّرُونَ﴾

﴾O believers! Do not enter houses other than your own until you obtain their permission. And greet their residents (immediately after you enter). This (advice) is better for you so that you may contemplate (its rationale).﴿[2]

3.4.6 Right of Equality

Furthermore, the right of security was also guaranteed by the Holy Prophet ﷺ, as well as human equality. Human equality was guaranteed by ensuring legal, social and economic equality (as far as the basic needs are concerned in the form of social and income support). The Holy Prophet ﷺ declared:

«لَا فَضْلَ لِعَرَبِيٍّ عَلَى أَعْجَمِيٍّ، وَلَا لِعَجَمِيٍّ عَلَى عَرَبِيٍّ، وَلَا لِأَحْمَرَ عَلَى أَسْوَدَ، وَلَا أَسْوَدَ عَلَى أَحْمَرَ إِلَّا بِالتَّقْوَى».

No Arab is superior to a non-Arab, and no non-Arab is superior to an Arab; no red person has a

[1] Related by al-Bukhārī in *al-Ṣaḥīḥ*, vol. 2, p. 834 §2236; Muslim in *al-Ṣaḥīḥ*, vol. 4, p. 1760 §2242; al-Dārīmī in *al-Sunan*, vol. 2, p. 426 §2814; and al-Bayhaqī in *al-Sunan al-Kubrā*, vol. 5, p. 214 §9851.

[2] Qur'ān 24:27.

> superiority over a black person, and no black person has superiority over a red person, except for those who are God-fearing.[1]

That is to say that superiority is based only on the character and moral integrity of a person, not on one's race, religion, or colour.

3.4.7 GUARANTEE OF LEGAL JUSTICE

Another constitutional guarantee provided by Islam through the Holy Qur'ān and through the Holy Prophet ﷺ, was the guarantee of legal justice.

The Qur'ān states:

﴿وَإِذَا حَكَمْتُم بَيْنَ ٱلنَّاسِ أَن تَحْكُمُوا۟ بِٱلْعَدْلِ﴾

﴾And when you judge matters among people, give judgment with justice.﴿[2]

This guarantee of legal equality and justice is an absolute statement of the Qur'ān and there is no mentioning of faith or religion. Thus, it is a universal right for the whole of mankind. Likewise, it is stated:

﴿إِنَّ ٱللَّهَ يَأْمُرُكُمْ أَن تُؤَدُّوا۟ ٱلْأَمَٰنَٰتِ إِلَىٰٓ أَهْلِهَا﴾

﴾Surely, Allah commands you to entrust the belongings to those who are worthy of them.﴿[3]

This is a general commandment that states whenever you are appointed or given an authority to adjudicate a matter,

---

[1] Related by Aḥmad b. Ḥanbal in *al-Musnad*, vol. 5, p. 411; Ibn al-Mubārak in *al-Musnad*, p. 147 §239; and Haythamī in *Majma' al-Zawā'id*, vol. 3, p. 266.

[2] Qur'ān 4:58.

[3] Qur'ān 4:58.

you are required to administer justice fairly regardless of the person's religion.

The Qur'ān states:

﴿يَـٰٓأَيُّهَا ٱلَّذِينَ ءَامَنُوا۟ كُونُوا۟ قَوَّٰمِينَ بِٱلْقِسْطِ شُهَدَآءَ لِلَّهِ وَلَوْ عَلَىٰٓ أَنفُسِكُمْ أَوِ ٱلْوَٰلِدَيْنِ وَٱلْأَقْرَبِينَ ۚ إِن يَكُنْ غَنِيًّا أَوْ فَقِيرًا فَٱللَّهُ أَوْلَىٰ بِهِمَا ۖ﴾

"O believers! Become tenaciously firm on justice, bearing witness (merely) for the sake of Allah even if (the witness) is against your own selves or (your) parents or (your) relatives. Whether the person (against whom is the evidence) is rich or poor, Allah is a greater Well-Wisher of them both (than you are)."[1]

That is to say that one has to administer justice on this earth and to become a witness to Almighty Allah.

3.4.8 Guarantee of Free-Trial

The guarantee of a hearing and a free-trial was given to every person and nobody would be punished without a proper, independent hearing, this also included the right of defence. Furthermore, freedom and liberty were also guaranteed; these concepts of human liberty and freedom were implemented many centuries later in other civilizations but these were promulgated, practiced, and enforced by Islam in the 7th Century.

3.4.9 Defence of the State of Medina

Interestingly, if one was to observe the first ten years of the Holy Prophet's life in Medina as head of the state up to the

---

[1] Qur'ān 4:135.

point of the conquest of Mecca, one would note that no war was fought on the borders of Mecca. All wars were imposed on the society of Medina and were fought on the borders of Medina, or within close proximity of the city-state. The first major battle was Badr in which there was an advancement and aggression by the Meccans. The second major battle was Uḥud which was fought at a distance of two miles away from Medina. Another major battle was the 'Battle of the Trench' which was fought on the very borders of Medina, when a trench was prepared to defend the city-state. Within those years there was no advancement or war of aggression by the Holy Prophet ﷺ until after the Treaty of Ḥudaybiya, when a ten year no-war pact was made with the Meccans in the 6th year of Hegira. However, after a year, the Meccans broke the contract. So the Prophet ﷺ made an advancement to conquer Mecca, which he did without shedding a single drop of blood.

When the Muslims had entered the city as conquerors, one of the Companions, Ansarite commander Saᶜd b. ᶜIbāda ؓ declared vehemently, 'today is the day of revenge.' For almost two decades, the Muslims had suffered under the hands of the Meccans and were forced to abandon their homes. So, the desire to exact revenge on their former oppressors was a natural reaction on that historic occasion. Emotions were running high, but when the Holy Prophet ﷺ heard his Companion's calling for retribution, he stood up and addressed the whole of Mecca and said:

«اَلْيَومُ يَومُ الْـمَرْحَمَةِ».

> (No! Today is not the day of revenge:) Today is the day of mercy and forgiveness.[1]

The Holy Prophet ﷺ forgave and pardoned his enemies and

[1] Related by Ibn Ḥajar al-ᶜAsqalānī in *Fatḥ al-Bārī*, vol. 8, pp. 8, 9; and Ibn ᶜAbd al-Barr in *al-Istīᶜāb*, vol. 2, p. 163.

set a precedent that was to be the distinctive hallmark of Islam from then on. The Holy Prophet ﷺ said:

«مَنْ دَخَلَ دَارَ أَبِي سُفْيَانَ فَهُوَ آمِنٌ، وَمَنْ أَلْقَى السِّلَاحَ فَهُوَ آمِنٌ، وَمَنْ أَغْلَقَ بَابَهُ فَهُوَ آمِنٌ».

> Whoever enters Abū Sufyān's house will attain security and whoever lays aside his arms will attain security and whoever shuts his gate will attain security.[1]

Unfortunately, and it is a matter of great shame that some criminals in our time have brought about a bad name to Islam through their own criminal activities and out of their own political agenda. Whilst at the same time the mistakes have been committed from the other side too, through their actions and foreign policies. There is a great misunderstanding between the West and Islam. If the true face of Islam is identified and its true teachings properly understood, then much progress would be made towards the restoration of world peace, as well as reconciliation and co-operation between the two civilizations. Terrorists have no religion, nor do they have any attachment to culture; they have no faith and are enemies of humanity, as well as the enemies of Islam.

---

[1] Related by Muslim in *al-Ṣaḥīḥ*, vol. 3, p. 1407 §1780; Ab‰ Dāw‰d in *al-Sunan*, vol. 3, p. 162 §3021; and al-Bazzār in *al-Musnad*, vol. 4, p. 122 §1292.

Part Three B

Al-Hidayah Europe 2009: Question & Answer Session (UK)

Q1. Regarding whether Terrorism is Caused by Factors within Islam or outside Islam

Dr Tahir Abbas (Director of the Centre for the Study of Ethnicity and Culture, University of Birmingham): Shaykh-ul-Islam, thank you for that very significant presentation. I'd like to draw your attention to the issues of the contemporary period. You highlighted towards the end that how those who allude to terrorism and use the name of Islam are criminals, they have subverted classical teachings. I'd like you to elaborate on when you think that began to go wrong: is it a function of internal problems or are the external policy dilemmas more of an issue? Please can you elaborate?

Shaykh-ul-Islam Dr Muhammad Tahir-ul-Qadri: This is a very interesting question to which I would like to give a brief answer. In my opinion this is not just an internal matter. This kind of terrorism has emerged out of an international political agenda. I was born in Pakistan, I spent my whole life there, and there were no acts of terrorism in Pakistan 20–25 years before: there were Muslims, there were religious institutions, and there were mosques, but we never came across any suicidal bombings, or any acts of terrorism. This developed when a sponsored war was fought against the illegal occupation of Afghanistan by Russia. At that time a global power wanted to fight against the Russian occupation and so certain people from the Arab world and in Afghanistan were sponsored: they were provided with arms and ammunition, money and training. That was the time when Osama Bin Laden became one of the heroes and that was the time when the Taliban came into existence.

This sponsored war against Russian occupation was fought, forcing the Russians to leave the land of Afghanistan. Then the sponsors left these terrorists to their own devices. They were then utilized to carry out their terroristic activities in Kashmir. When they were banned from fighting in Kashmir, they started to spread in Pakistan and they had nothing to do except killing, because this was the skill which they were taught. So I think a political global agenda was the basis for the emergence of terrorism: these terrorists in Pakistan have advanced arms and logistics which even the Pakistani army does not possess, as well as money (to carry out their activities). The question is where do they get all of this from? How did Baitullah Mehsud become a giant from just an ordinary person? How did the Taliban become giants from just ordinary students of *madrasas*?

To eliminate them we have to decide whether elimination of terrorism is our humanistic agenda or our expansionistic agenda. I think, sincerely and honestly, if eradication and elimination of terrorism from the whole world is our humanistic agenda, then elimination of terrorism is not a matter of 1 to 2 years, but if it is a political and expansionistic agenda then it will continue for the whole century.

Q2. Regarding the Prospect of Muslims Supporting Terrorism

Phil Rees (prominent journalist and producer): Hello Shaykh-ul-Islam, thank you for inviting me here. I covered the war in Afghanistan in the 1980s and later of course the war in Bosnia and in both cases, Muslims felt a duty to help their brothers and sisters in distress. I think everyone here will know the hadith of course, of the 'one body' when one part of the body is ill the whole body feels ill. At that time, I remember coming up to Coventry, people were raising money for people in Bosnia who were suffering and it would seem as a very proud thing to do, a proper thing to do; obviously to do that now would be considered an act of terrorism where there are foreign armies occupying *Dār al-Islām*, or at least have their presence there. How would you see the two and compare the two in terms of duty of Muslims to help their brothers?

Shaykh-ul-Islam Dr Muhammad Tahir-ul-Qadri: Thank you, I understand and agree with you that the whole of the Muslim Umma is like a body, but remember there are different organs to that body. Working as a body, no doubt that it is required in Islam and it has been practiced in the past, but at the same time if a single organ of that body becomes cancerous then the other organs are not supposed to support that cancer, instead they will support the surgeon to cut this cancerous organ off! Because by doing so the whole body will be protected from the spreading of that cancer.

Terrorism is no less than a cancer: if any part of the Muslim world or any group begins terrorist activities, it means that there is a cancer in this body of Muslims. So, the Muslims are compulsorily required to help the surgeon to remove that part of the body so that the remaining portion of the body is safe. That is why terrorist activities can never be supported by any Muslim, even if the terrorists abuse the name of jihad.

Jihad is never an act of terrorism: jihad is to fight against terrorism. The concept of jihad is a struggle, a sacred struggle, against the evil desires of our lower self. Jihad is a sacred struggle to spread knowledge and to remove ignorance within society. Jihad is a sacred struggle for charity, to remove any economic unbalance and to fight against poverty and to bring about its elimination. Jihad is a sacred struggle to free and liberate people from acts of oppression like the injustices of Saddam or the Taliban who have given a really bad name to Islam. The Muslims as a body should never support a cancerous organ. We have to differentiate between what is right and what is wrong.

Q3. Regarding the Misuse of the Blasphemy Law against Pakistani Christians

Canon Dr Christopher Lamb (representative of Archbishop of Canterbury Dr Rowan Williams): Shaykh... I would like to echo the thanks of others to the invitation.

Shaykh-ul-Islam Dr Muhammad Tahir-ul-Qadri: You're welcome. You know many Christian scholars and bishops in Pakistan, such as Dr Andrew Francis and Dr Azaria who are the representatives of the Catholic Church; I always invite them, and we celebrate Christmas every year at our (Central) Secretariat, (Lahore); and we always open our mosque for our Christian brothers to worship according to their faith - this is our practice. So you should feel at home; you are not our guest, you may consider yourself as the host of this session!

Canon Dr Christopher Lamb: Shukriya (thank-you), I do indeed feel at home and you mentioned the Christians of Pakistan, it's them who I have in mind. I'm thankful for your words about freedom of religion in Islam and freedom to believe and not to be compelled otherwise. There is, however, a problem in Pakistan which you will be familiar with, in the operation of the blasphemy law which on a number of occasions very recently has caused considerable trouble for Christians when false allegations have been made that the Qur'ān has been defaced or spoiled in some way. Only 10 days ago, 30 Christian homes were destroyed and people killed and the fire fighters were prevented from going to help those people. It must also be said that there were Muslims who helped the Christians in that situation, but I wanted to ask you about the operation of the blasphemy law which has been misused and exploited both against Christians and also against fellow Muslims, and I wonder really about the wisdom of it.

Shaykh-ul-Islam Dr Muhammad Tahir-ul-Qadri: Thank you, I agree with your concern, I absolutely agree with your concern, but let me explain. You know the law is of two kinds: one is the substantive aspect of law and the other is the procedural aspect of law. When we talk of the law of blasphemy; there is nothing wrong as far as the substantive aspect of the law is concerned. I as a student of Law, having been a professor of Law throughout my career - I can say that there is nothing wrong with regards to the substantive aspect of the law. When you use the word 'misuse' it makes the case clear. The wrong which we see is in the procedural aspect of the law. This is not a law against the Christian community, this is a matter of corruption in the police force.

The problem is that the corrupt police officers are used to taking bribes. They don't just register cases wrongly against Christians, they register cases against poor Muslims too, either under the pressure of the landlords, or under the pressure of the MNAs and MPAs ("members of national and provincial assemblies") and other influential political figures. They register the case of theft against people. This is a misuse of the law of theft; they register the case of fornication against people - this is a misuse of the law of adultery; there are hundreds and thousands of cases being registered in police stations everyday against poor and weak people. So every law is being misused whether in its original sense it was correct or wrong, every single law is being misused. Even the constitution is being misused by military dictators and they take over the charge. The influential people always misuse the laws, because there is no proper administration of justice, and the people working as police officers are not like those who are the police officers of British society and the Western world. There is a hell of a difference between the Pakistani police officer and the British police officer. So, the basic thing is to stop the misuse of law because there is no problem with the law itself. Some amendments according to me are necessarily required in procedural law.

I support that every police officer in the police station should not be allowed to register a case against any non-Muslim. The authority to trial any law of blasphemy should be given to a single magistrate in the district and after full scrutiny the case should go on trial; no police officer should be authorised to trial or investigate the cases. Only the men of integrity should be authorised to trial the case, so that they are also safe and the same kind of administration of justice should be applied to poor members of Pakistani society. This is a matter of corruption, not a matter of religion.

Q4. Regarding advice to Western Governments

Maqsood Ahmed (Senior Advisor from Communities Ministry): Al-Salām-u ʿAlaykum Qibla Ḥuzūr, Shaykh-ul-Islam. I have been listening to you this morning and this afternoon as well. I think what I hear from yourself and from the hall is the voice of reason and moderation, but our difficulty in the British community and the British Muslim community is that we don't have many voices of reason. Looking at your eminent colleague Dr Safarāz Naʿīmī (and his martyrdom) who gave that same voice of reason as you are giving; those voices are silenced by the terrorists. How could you advise us to help to raise the voice of reason? *Jazāk Allāh Khayr.*

Shaykh-ul-Islam Dr Muhammad Tahir-ul-Qadri: My brief advice on this subject is that I would like to ask the global authorities and the global powers, please, please, and please, don't help the friends of terrorists, just help the friends of peace.

I know in Pakistan as well as in the other parts of the world, there are people who are very clever and who work very closely with the British and Western European governments, but they may have some close relationship with those parties and groups who have extreme ideas, and those groups who have very extreme ideas are closely linked with the terrorists, and they are known to be the friends and reliable persons and colleagues of the Western and British governments. So, you have to discriminate between friends and enemies. This is my only advice.

I think up till now the Western world has not been able to discriminate between their real friends and their real enemies. The day when they will discriminate between their real friends and their real enemies in connection to the war against terrorism, *in shā Allāh*, the war against terrorism will definitively reach the stage of success.

Q5. Regarding a Research Path to Follow for Promoting the Positive Coexistence of Muslims in UK Society

Dr Sophie Gilliat-Ray, Director, Centre for the Study of Islam in the UK, Cardiff University: Thank you very much indeed for this opportunity to address a question to you. In the research centre that I direct at Cardiff University, our underlining mission is the promotion of understanding of Islam and the life of Muslims in Britain. And we work in a very close partnership with the local Muslim community and the Muslim council of Wales in trying to fulfil that ambition. I'm not an Islamic scholar but I am academic and I would really like your advice based on your engagement with British Muslims and your understanding of the situation in relation to Islam in Britain. What do you think is the most important priority for a research centre such as mine at Cardiff University?

Shaykh-ul-Islam Dr Muhammad Tahir-ul-Qadri: Thank you, I think the most effective and influential role to be played by the research centre is to promote the real and correct concept of integration. There are three models that a minority can adopt within a larger society such as Britain. These three models are the model of isolation, the model of annihilation/assimilation, and the model of integration.

There are some Muslims who consider themselves to be practicing and devout, but love to remain in the model of isolation. You have to produce research in order to develop their understanding that living in isolation and not interacting with the wider community is totally against the teachings of Islam, as well as going against the general ethos of being a member of society; it is important that they understand that being part and parcel of British society is absolutely in accordance with the teachings of Islam. So, they have to come out, and you have to help to bring them out of isolation. This would be the message for the religious people and Muslims in general.

And, on the other hand, you have to promote research for the British government stating that bringing them out from isolation does not mean that they have to adopt the model of annihilation or assimilation. The research should try to address the issue that the model of isolation will be damaging for the Muslims, whilst on the other hand, the model of annihilation will be damaging for British society. Annihilation is never a good model because every culture has its own roots and identity; and every culture has its own traits and attributes. So, when you take them out from isolation, you have to ensure at the same time that you protect them from the annihilation model, because this will create a reaction. So, your research should follow these lines.

The best future for British society is indeed the model of integration. What does it mean? Integration is the full and active participation of minorities within society with a guaranteed protection of their cultural identity, as well as their religious identity. If this path is adopted then this will lead to a multicultural society, and then finally this multiculturalism itself will become a culture! So your research, your seminars, and your printed material should aim to give a message to both sides: one to the Muslims arguing the case that you have to come out of isolation and become part and parcel of British society; and on the other hand a message should go to the governments to warn them of the pitfalls in the model of annihilation or assimilation, by telling policy makers and politicians alike that they should not advance policies that subdue the identity of minorities. This will hopefully lead to the development of integration. If this model of integration is carried out successfully then British society will indeed be one of the most prosperous societies. I do believe that the British society is one of the best societies of the Western world; it is a multicultural society. Since I am a Canadian citizen, I would say that my Canadian society is in fact the best in the world, but at the same time I can see that Britain is also working on the same lines. So the protection of the splendour and diversity of British society, and its value, lies in multiculturalism; and multiculturalism can only be protected through integration. This is the work that needs to be done. Thank You.

Bibliography

al-Qur'ān

Exegesis of the Qur'ān

al-Qurṭubī, Abū ʿAbd Allāh Muhammad b. Aḥmad b. Abī Bakr (d. 671 AH), *al-Jāmiʿ li-Aḥkām al-Qur'ān*, Cario, Egypt: Dār al-Shuʿab, 1372 AH.

Hadith Collections

ʿAbd al-Razzāq, Abū Bakr b. al-Hammām b. al-Nāfiʿ al-Ṣanʿānī (126–211/744–826), *al-Muṣannaf*, Beirut, Lebanon: al-Maktab al-Islamī, 1403 AH.

Aḥmad b. Ḥanbal, Abū ʿAbd Allāh b. Muhammad (164–241/780–855), *al-Musnad*, Beirut, Lebanon: al-Maktab al-Islamī, 1398/1978.

al-Bayhaqī, Abū Bakr Aḥmad b. al-Ḥusayn (384–458/994–1066), *Shuʿab al-Īmān*, Beirut, Lebanon: Dār al-Kutub al-ʿIlmiyya, 1410/1990.

—. *as-Sunan al-Kubrā*, Makka, Saudi Arabia: Maktaba Dār al-Bāz, 1414/1994.

al-Bazzār, Abū Bakr Aḥmad b. ʿAmr b. ʿAbd al-Khāliq al-Baṣrī (210–292/825–905), *al-Musnad*, Beirut, Lebanon: Mu'assisa ʿUlūm al-Qur'ān, 1409 AH.

al-Bukhārī, Abū ʿAbd Allāh Muhammad b. Ismāʿīl b. Ibrāhīm (194–256/810–870), *al-Ṣaḥīḥ*, Beirut, Lebanon: Dār Ibn Kathīr, al-Yamāma, 1407/1987.

—. *al-Adab al-Mufrad*, Damascus, Syria: Dār al-Qalam, 1st ed. 1422/2001.

al-Dāraquṭnī, Abū al-Ḥasan ʿAlī b. ʿUmar (306–385/918–995), *al-Sunan*, Beirut, Lebanon: ʿĀlim al-Kutub, 4th ed. 1406/1986.

—. *al-Sunan*, Beirut, Lebanon: Dār al-Maʿrifa, 1386/1966.

al-Dārimī, Abū Muhammad ʿAbd Allāh (181–255/797–869), *al-Sunan*, Beirut, Lebanon: Dār al-Kitāb al-ʿArabī, 1407 AH.

al-Daylamī, Abū Shujāʿ Shīrawayh b. Shardār b. Shīrawayh (445–509/1053–1115), *Musnad al-Firdaws*, Beirut, Lebanon: Dār al-Kutub al-ʿIlmiyya, 1406/1986.

Abū Dāwūd, Sulaymān b. Ashʿath (202–275/817–889), *al-Sunan*, Beirut, Lebanon: Dār al-Fikr, 1414/1994.

al-Ḥākim, Abū ʿAbd Allāh Muhammad b. ʿAbd Allāh b. Muhammad (321–405/933–1014), *al-Mustadrak ʿalā al-Ṣaḥīḥayn,* Beirut, Lebanon: Dār al-Kutub al-ʿIlmiyya, 1411/1990.

al-Haythamī, Nūr al-Dīn Abu al-Ḥasan ʿAlī b. Abī Bakr (735–807/1335–1405), *Majmaʿ al-Zawāʾid,* Cairo, Egypt: Dār ar-Riyān li-t-Turāth & Beirut Lebanon: Dār al-Kitab al-ʿArabī, 1407/1987.

Ibn Ḥibbān, Abū Ḥātim Muhammad b. Ḥibbān b. Aḥmad b. Ḥibbān (270–354/884–965), *al-Ṣaḥīḥ*, Beirut, Lebanon: Muʾassisa al-Risālah, 2nd ed. 1414/1993.

al-Hindī, ʿAlā al-Dīn ʿAlī al-Muttaqī b. Ḥassām al-Dīn (d. 975 AH), *Kanz al-ʿUmmāl fī Sunan al-Afʿāl wa al-Aqwāl*, Beirut, Lebanon: Muʾassisa al-Risāla, 2nd ed. 1399/1979.

Ibn Khuzayma, Abū Bakr Muhammad b. Isḥāq (223–311/838–924), *al-Ṣaḥīḥ,* Beirut, Lebanon: al-Maktab al-Islamī, 1390/1970.

al-Marwazī, Abū Bakr Aḥmad b. ʿAlī b. Saʿīd al-Umawī (d. 202–292 AH), *Musnad Abī Bakr al-Ṣiddīq,* Beirut, Lebanon: al-Maktab al-Islamī.

Ibn Mājah, Muhammad b. Yazīd (209–273/824–887), *al-Sunan*, Beirut, Lebanon: Dār al-Kutub al-ʿIlmiyya, 1st ed. 1419/1998.

—. *al-Sunan*, Beirut, Lebanon: Dār al-Fikr.

Mālik, Ibn Anas b. Mālik b. Abī ʿĀmir b. ʿAmr b. al-Ḥārith al-Aṣbaḥī (93–179/712–795), *al-Muwaṭṭaʾ*, Beirut, Lebanon: Dār Iḥyāʾ at-Turāth al-ʿArabī, 1406/1985.

Ibn Manda, Abū ʿAbd Allāh Muhammad b. Isḥāq (310–395/922–1005), *al-Īmān*, Beirut, Lebanon: Muʾassisa al-Risāla, 2nd ed. 1406 AH.

Ibn al-Mubārak, Abū ʿAbd al-Raḥmān ʿAbd Allāh b. Wāḍ iḥ al-Marwazī (118–181/736–798), *Kitāb al-Zuhd*, Beirut, Lebanon: Dār al-Kutub al-ʿIlmiyya.

Muslim, Ibn al-Ḥajjāj al-Qushayrī (206–261/821–875), *al-Ṣaḥīḥ*, Beirut, Lebanon: Dār Ihyāʾ al-Turāth al-ʿArabī, n.d.

an-Nasāʾī, Aḥmad b. Shuʿayb Abū ʿAbd al-Raḥmān (215–303/830–915), *al-Sunan*, Beirut, Lebanon: Dār al-Kutub al-ʿIlmiyya, 1416/1995 & Ḥalb, Syria: Maktab al-Maṭbūʿāt al-Islamiyya, 1406/1986.

—. *al-Sunan al-Kubrā*, Beirut, Lebanon: Dār al-Kutub al-ʿIlmiyya, 1411/1991.

Abū Nuʿaym, Aḥmad b. ʿAbd Allāh b. Aḥmad b. Isḥāq al-Aṣbahānī (336–430/948–1038), *Musnad al-Imām Abī Ḥanīfa*, Riyadh, Saudi Arabia, Maktabat al-Kawthar, 1415 AH.

al-Qaḍāʿī, Abū ʿAbd Allāh Muhammad b. Salama b. Jaʿfar b. ʿAlī (d. 454/1062), *Musnad al-Shihāb*, Beirut, Lebanon: Muʾassisa al-Risāla, 1407 AH.

al-Shāfiʿī, Abū ʿAbd Allāh Muhammad b. Idrīs (150–204/767–819), *al-Musnad*, Beirut, Lebanon: Dār al-Kutub al-ʿIlmiyya, 1st ed. 1400/1980.

al-Shāshī, Abū Saʿīd Haytham (d. 335/946 AH), *al-Musnad*, Medina, Saudi Arabia, Maktaba al-ʿUlūm wa al-Ḥikam, 1410 AH.

Ibn Abī Shayba, Abū Bakr ʿAbd Allāh b. Muhammad b. Ibrāhīm (159–235/776–850), *al-Muṣannaf*, Riyadh, Saudi Arabia: Maktaba al-Rushd, 1409 AH.

al-Ṭabarānī, Sulaymān b. Aḥmad (260–360/873–971), *al-Muʿjam al-Awsaṭ*, Cairo, Egypt: Dār al-Ḥaramayn, 1415 AH.

—. *al-Muʿjam al-Kabīr*, Beirut, Lebanon: Dār Ihyāʾ al-Turāth al-ʿArabī, n.d.

—. *al-Muʿjam al-Kabīr*, Mosul, Iraq: Maktaba al-ʿUlūm wa al-Ḥikam, 1403/1983.

al-Tirmidhī, Abū ʿĪsā Muhammad b. ʿĪsā (210–279/825–892), *al-Sunan*, Beirut, Lebanon: Dār al-Fikr, n.d.

—. *al-Sunan*, Beirut, Lebanon: Dār al-Iḥyāʾ at-Turāth.

Abū Yaʿlā, Aḥmad b. ʿAlī al-Mūṣilī al-Tamīmī (210–307/825–919), *al-Musnad*, Damascus, Syria: Dār al-Maʾmūn li-t-Turāth, 1404/1984.

al-Zaylaʿī, Abū Muhammad ʿAbd Allāh b. Yūsuf al-Ḥanafī (d. 762/1360), *Naṣb al-Rāya li-Aḥadīth al-Hidāya,* Egypt: Dār al-Ḥadīth, 1357/1938.

Hadith Commentaries

Ibn Ḥajar al-ʿAsqalānī, Aḥmad b. ʿAlī b. Muhammad b. Muhammad b. ʿAlī b. Aḥmad al-Kinānī (773–852/1372–1449), *Fatḥ al-Bārī Sharḥ Ṣaḥīḥ al-Bukarī,* Beirut, Lebanon, Dār al-Maʿrifa, 1379 AH.

Ibn Rajab al-Ḥanbalī, Abū al-Faraj ʿAbd al-Raḥmān b. Aḥmad (736–795 AH), *Jāmiʿ al-ʿUlūm wa al-Ḥikam fī Sharḥ Khamsīn Ḥadīth min Jawāmiʿ al-Kalim*, Beirut, Lebanon: Dār al-Maʿrifa, 1408 AH.

Biography of Hadith Narrators

Ibn ʿAbd al-Barr, Abū ʿUmar Yūsuf b. ʿAbd Allāh b. Muhammad (368–463/979–1071), *al-Istīʿāb fī Maʿrifa al-Aṣḥāb*, Beirut, Lebanon: Dār al-Kutub al-ʿIlmiyya, 2nd ed. 1422/2002.

al-Mizzī, Abū al-Ḥajjāj Yūsuf b. Zakī ʿAbd al-Raḥmān b. Yūsuf (654–742/1256–1341), *Tahdhīb al-Kamāl*, Beirut, Lebanon: Muʾassisa al-Risāla, 1400/1980.

Jurisprudence

Ibn Ḥazm, ʿAlī b. Aḥmad b. Saʿīd ibn Ḥazm al-Andalusī (383–456/993–1064), *al-Muḥallā*, Beirut, Lebanon: Dār al-Fikr, n.d.

—. *al-Muḥallā*, Beirut, Lebanon: Dār al-Āfāq al-Jadīda.

al-Kāsānī, Abū Bakr (d. 587 AH), *Badāʾiʿ al-Ṣanāʾiʿ*, Karachi, Pakistan: H. M. Saʿīd Co. 1st ed. 1328/1910.

—. *Badāʾiʿ al-Ṣanāʾiʿ*, Beirut, Lebanon: Dār al-Kitab al-ʿArabī, 1982 AD.

Ibn al-Qayyim, Abū ʿAbd Allāh Muhammad b. Abī Bakr Ayyūb al-Zarʿī (691–751/1292–1350), *Aḥkām Ahl al-Dhimma*, Beirut, Lebanon: Dār Ibn Ḥazm, 1418/1997.

Ibn Qudāma, Abū Muhammad ʿAbd Allāh b. Aḥmad al-Maqdisī (d. 620 AH), *al-Mughnī fī Fiqh al-Imām Aḥmad b. Ḥanbal al-Shaybānī*, Riyadh, Saudi Arabia: Maktaba al-Riyāḍ al-Ḥaditha, n.d.

—. *al-Mughnī fī Fiqh al-Imām Aḥmad b. Ḥanbal al-Shaybānī*, Beirut, Lebanon: Dār al-Fikr, 1405 AH.

al-Shāfiʿī, Abū ʿAbd Allāh Muhammad b. Idrīs (150–204/767–819), *al-Umm*, Beirut, Lebanon: Dār al-Maʿrifa, 2nd ed. 1406/1986.

al-Shaybānī, Abū ʿAbd Allāh Muhammad b. al-Ḥasan (132–189 AH), *Kitāb al-Ḥujja*, Beirut, Lebanon: ʿĀlam al-Kutub, 1403 AH.

—. *Kitāb al-Ḥujja*, Lahore, Pakistan: Dār al-Maʿārif al-Nuʿmāniyya, n.d.

—. *al-Mabsūṭ*, Karachi, Pakistan: Idāra al-Qurʾān wa al-ʿUlūm, n.d.

al-Shawkānī, Muhammad b. ʿAlī b. Muhammad (1173–1250/1760–1834), *Nayl al-Awtār*, Beirut, Lebanon: Dār al-Jīl, 1973.

al-Shurbīnī, al-Shaykh Muhammad al-Khaṭīb (d. 977 AH), *Mughnī al-Muḥtāj*, Beirut, Lebanon: Dār ihyāʾ al-Turāth al-ʿArabī, n.d.

al-Ṭaḥāwī, Abū Jaʿfar Aḥmad b. Muhammad b. Salama (229–321/853–933), *Sharḥ Maʿānī al-Āthār*, Beirut, Lebanon: Dār al-Kutub al-ʿIlmiyya, 1399 AH.

Abū ʿUbayd al-Qāsim b. al-Sallām (d. 224 AH), *Kitāb al-Amwāl*, Cairo, Egypt: Maktaba al-Kulliyāt al-Azhariyya, 3rd ed. 1401/1981.

—. *Kitāb al-Amwāl*, Beirut, Lebanon: Dār al-Fikr, 1408 AH.

Abū Yūsuf, Yaʿqūb b. Ibrāhīm (d. 182 AH), *Kitāb al-Kharāj*, Beirut, Lebanon: Dār al-Maʿrifa, n.d.

—. *Kitāb al-Kharāj*, Lahore, Pakistan: al-Maktabat al-Islamiyya, 1974 AD.

Ibn Zanjuway, Ḥamīd (251 AH), *Kitāb al-Amwāl*, Beirut, Lebanon: ʿĀlim al-Kutub, 1403 AH.

PROPHETIC BIOGRAPHY

al-Bayhaqī, Abū Bakr Aḥmad b. al-Ḥusayn (384–458/994–1066), *Dalāʾil al-Nubuwwa*, Beirut, Lebanon: Dār al-Kutub al-ʿIlmiyya, 2nd ed. 1423/2002.

Ibn Hishām, Abū Muhammad ʿAbd al-Malik (d. 213/828), *al-Sīra al-Nabawiyya*, Damascus, Syria: Dār al-Kalim al-Ṭayyab, 1st ed. 1420/1999.

—. *al-Sīra al-Nabawiyya*, Beirut, Lebanon: Dār al-Jīl, 1st ed. 1411.

al-Qasṭallānī, Abū al-ʿAbbās Aḥmad b. Muhammad b. Abī Bakr b. ʿAbd al-Malik (851–923/1448–1517), *al-Mawāhib al-Laduniyya bi al-Minḥ al-Muhammadiyya*, Beirut, Lebanon: al-Maktab al-Islamī, 1412/1991.

Ibn al-Qayyim, Abū ʿAbd Allāh Muhammad b. Abū Bakr Ayyū al-Zaraʿī al-Jawziyya (691–751/1292–1350), *Zād al-Maʿād*, Beirut, Lebanon: Muʾassisa al-Risāla, 8th ed. 1405/1985.

Ibn Saʿd, Abū ʿAbd Allāh Muhammad (168–230/784–845), *al-Ṭabaqāt al-Kubrā*, Beirut, Lebanon: Dār Beirut li al-Ṭabāʿat wa al-Nashr, 1398/1978.

al-Ṣāliḥī, Muhammad b. Yūsuf al-Shāmī (d. 942/1536), *Subul al-Hudā wa al-Rishād*, Beirut, Lebanon: Dār al-Kutub al-ʿIlmiyya, 1414/1993.

Ibn Sayyid al-Nās, Abū al-Fatḥ Muhammad (671–734 AH), *ʿUyūn al-Athar fī Funūn al-Maghāzī wa al-Shamāʾil wa al-Siyar*, Beirut, Lebanon: Dār al-Qalam, 1414/1993.

al-Suhaylī, Abū al-Qāsim ʿAbd al-Raḥmān b. ʿAbd Allāh (508–581 AH), *al-Rawḍ al-Unuf*, Beirut, Lebanon: Dār al-Kutub al-ʿIlmiyya, 1418/1997.

Ibn Taymiyya, Aḥmad b. ʿAbd al-Ḥalīm b. ʿAbd al-Salām al-Ḥarānī (661–728/1263–1328), *al-Ṣārim al-Maslūl*, Beirut, Lebanon, Dār Ibn Ḥazam, 1417 AH.

al-Zurqānī, Abū ʿAbd Allāh Muhammad b. ʿAbd al-Bāqī b. Yūsuf b. Aḥmad (1055–1122/1645–1710), *Sharḥ Mawāhib al-Laduniyya*, Beirut, Lebanon: Dār al-Kutub al-ʿIlmiyya, 1417/1996.

SUFISM

Abū Nuʿaym, Aḥmad b. ʿAbd Allāh b. Aḥmad b. Isḥāq al-Aṣbahānī (336–430/948–1038), *Ḥilyat al-Awliyāʾ wā Ṭabaqāt al-Aṣfiyāʾ*, Beirut, Lebanon: Dār al-Kitāb al-ʿArabī, 1405/1985.

HISTORY

Ibn ʿAsākir, Abū al-Qāsim ʿAlī b. al-Ḥasan b. Hibat Allāh b. ʿAbd Allāh al-Dimashqī (499–571/1105–1176), *Tārīkh*

Dimashq al-Kabīr (generally known as *Tārīkh Ibn ʿAsākīr)*, Beirut, Lebanon: Dār al-Fikr, 1995 AD.

al-Balādhurī, Aḥmad b. Yaḥyā b. Jābir b. Dāwūd (d. 289/892), *Futūḥ al-Buldān*, Beirut, Lebanon: Dār al-Kutub al-ʿIlmiyya, 1403/1983.

—. *Futūḥ al-Buldān*, Alexandria: Dār Ibn Khaldūn, n.d.

Ibn al-Jawzī, Abū al-Faraj ʿAbd al-Raḥmān b. ʿAlī b. Muhammad b. ʿAlī b. ʿUbayd Allāh (510–579/1116–1201), *al-Muntaẓim fī Tārīkh al Mumlūk wa al-Umam*, Beirut, Lebanon: Dār al-Kutub al-ʿIlmiyya, 1409/1989.

Ibn Kathīr, Abū al-Fidāʾ Ismāʿīl b. ʿUmar (701–774/1301–1373), *al-Bidāya wa al-Nihāya*, Beirut, Lebanon: Dār al-Fikr, 1419/1998.

—. *al-Bidāya wa al-Nihāya*, Beirut, Lebanon: Maktabat al-Maʿārif, n.d.

Ibn Khaldūn, ʿAbd al-Raḥmān b. Muhammad al-Ḥaḍramī (732–808 AH), *al-Tārīkh* (*History*), Beirut, Lebanon: Dār al-Qalam, 1984 AD.

al-Khaṭīb al-Baghdādī, Abū Bakr Aḥmad b. ʿAlī b. al-Thābit (393–463/1003–1071), *Tārīkh Baghdād*, Beirut, Lebanon: Dār al Kutāb al-ʿIlmiyya.

al-Ṭabarī, Abū Jaʿfar b. Jarīr Muhammad (224–310/839–923), *Tārīkh al-Umam wa al-Mulūk*, Beirut, Lebanon: Dār al-Kutub al-ʿIlmiyya, 1st ed. 1424/2001.

Linguistics

Ibn Fāris, Abū al-Ḥusayn Aḥmad b. Fāris b. Zakariyya al-Qazwīnī al-Rāzī (d. 395 AH), *Muʿjam Maqāyīs al-Lugha*, Beirut, Lebanon: Dār al-Jīl, 1420/1999.

Abū Manṣūr al-Azharī, Muhammad b. Aḥmad (282–370 AH), *Tahdhīb al-Lugha*.

Ibn Manẓūr, Muhammad b. Mukarram b. ʿAlī b. Aḥmad b. Abī Qāsim b. Ḥabqa al-Ifrīqī (630–711/1232–1311), *Lisān al-ʿArab*, Beirut, Lebanon: Dār Ṣādir.

BOOKS IN ENGLISH

Alan Brinkley, Frank Freidel, Richard Nelson Current, Harry T. Williams, *American History: A Survey*, New York, 7th Ed. 1987.

Cotterrell, Roger, *The Sociology of Law*, Butterworth's, London, 2nd ed. 1992.

Electioneering: A Comparative Study of Continuity and Change, Ed. by David Butler and Austin Ranney, Oxford: Clarendon Press, 1992.

Hart, James, *The American Presidency in Action 1789: A Study in Constitutional History*, New York: The Macmillan Company, 1948.

Jefferson, *Government by the People*, Prentice Hall, 15th ed. 1993.

Jolliffe, J. E. A., *The Constitutional History of Medieval England from the English Settlement to 1485*.

Knappen, M. M., *Constitutional and Legal History of England*, New York: Harcourt Brace, 1942.

Melvin I. Urofsky, Paul Finkelman, *A March of Liberty: A Constitutional History of the United States*, Oxford University Press, 2002.

Selected Documents of English Constitutional History, Ed. By George Burton Adams & H. Morse Stephens, London: Macmillan & Co. Ltd., 1901.